Cognitive Behavioral Therapy (CBT)

Reshape Your Brain to Eliminate Anxiety, Depression, and Negative Thoughts in Just 14 Days CBT Psychotherapy Proven Techniques & Exercises

Congratulations on purchasing Cognitive Behavioral Therapy (CBT): Reshape Your Brain to Eliminate Anxiety, Depression, and Negative Thoughts in Just 14 Days CBT Psychotherapy Proven Techniques & Exercises, and thank you for doing so!

The following chapters will discuss what the CBT is and make you learn the Most Effective CBT and DBT Techniques in order to Overcome Anxiety, Depression, Insomnia and will cover many more topics.

The information found in this book will best explore different exercises and techniques in order to successfully retrain your brain for your day to day life.

Thanks again for choosing this book! Every effort was made to ensure it is full of as much useful information as possible. Please enjoy!

Table of Contents

Chapter 1: Introduction to Cognitive
Behavioral Therapy 4

Chapter 2: The Mind with Cognitive
Behavioral Therapy 33

Chapter 3: Using Cognitive Behavioral
Therapy in Daily Life 55

Chapter 4: Cognitive Behavioral Therapy in
Action 82

Chapter 5: Dialectical Behavioral Therapy
in Action 106

Chapter 6: Benefiting from CBT and DBT in
Daily Life 119

Conclusion 128

Chapter 1: Introduction to Cognitive Behavioral Therapy

Many people are unaware of the term 'cognitive behavioral therapy.' Yet, most of us know some of the basic principles behind the process. But what is cognitive behavioral therapy?

Firstly, cognitive behavioral therapy is often shortened to 'CBT' for ease. This type of therapy was inspired by the cognitive theory common in the study of mental illnesses. This field, psychopathology, studies the effects of mental illness on our psyche and behavior.

The cognitive model, also known as the cognitive theory explains that emotions greatly cause or lead to our actions. This means that our spontaneous thoughts or perceptions in any given situation affect our emotions and therefore our behaviors. For instance, if we begin to think and believe *"I don't deserve happiness"*, then we can self-sabotage so that we never attain happiness.

Our perceptions of a situation and ourselves can often become dysfunctional and even distorted when we are upset or stressed. As this occurs, we can begin to think that the negative thoughts that pop into our minds, otherwise known as automatic thoughts are correct. If we are stressed about not being able to accomplish a task on time, our thoughts can turn to self-negative thoughts. Before long, we can begin to believe that these thoughts are correct and that we are a failure.

Cognitive behavioral therapy focuses on correcting these negative false thoughts and perceptions. By doing so, we are able to greatly decrease stress and begin to live a healthier and happier life. Anxiety is known to decrease, depression improves, insomnia lessens, and many other symptoms can see either improvement or completely go away.

In a nutshell, with cognitive behavioral therapy, we can learn to recognize our perceptions that have been distorted. These perceptions may be of ourselves, other people, or even the world we live in. The distorted perceptions influence our thoughts, reactions, and all of the information that we process. Therefore, the cognitive model taught by CBT aids us in mediating our responses by first correcting our thought process.

Sigmund Freud believed that behavior and mental illness largely stems from our childhood. Instead, the cognitive model teaches that these behaviors stem from our thoughts and perceptions. Some of these perceptions may have been created during childhood. For instance, if someone was bullied, they may have also been created during adulthood. Either way, our false perceptions can greatly impact our lives without us realizing.

To help us learn to overcome our false perceptions, therapists will use a process known as Socratic questioning. This questioning process helps us to evaluate ourselves, our thoughts, and situations. This will help us learn to find which thoughts are false and develop a healthier thought process. But, while therapists fully know what Socratic questioning is, most people who have not studied psychology are at a loss when they hear the term. This questioning process is actually quite simple and easy.

You may have guessed from the term 'Socratic questioning' but the term originates from the famed Greek philosopher, Socrates. When teaching his students, Socrates developed a method of questioning which would allow the students to closely evaluate a matter and then determine its validity and the truth. While Socrates most likely didn't intend for his questioning method to have such a profound impact on psychology and therapy, there is no doubt of how effective it has been.

Questions such as *"how else can I look at this,"*

"what has led me to believe this," "why do I think this happened," and *"have I considered the other person's perspective."* All of these questions, along with a number of others, can help us reach a different and healthier conclusion.

By utilizing these Socratic questioning in everyday life, we can learn to overcome our negative and incorrect thoughts. We can better analyze ourselves and our insecurities. For instance, imagine you are at work and were unable to attain a deadline. Because of this, your boss became upset which led you to believe that you are bad at your job.

The first thing you should do is to ask yourself why you are feeling this way. The reason could either be because you failed to meet your deadline or because your boss became upset. After you isolate the reason why you are feeling a certain way, you need to question whether or not genuine evidence proves these thoughts. Most likely, they aren't.

After you come to the realization that you aren't bad at your job, you can question what led you to feel this way. What impacted your perspective? Once you understand what is influencing your perspective, you can come to terms with it and create a new healthier and accurate perception.

For instance, maybe the reason that your boss

became upset with you wasn't because you are bad at your job, but because they themselves are stressed. They maybe are having a bad day because of work or because of other circumstances in their life.

The reason could have also been because you didn't meet your deadline. There are different possibilities for what could have caused this and isolating the reason can help. If you find the reason was that you were working on a project that you didn't have sufficient experience with, then you can take it as a learning experience. If you didn't have enough help or your boss didn't give you enough time on the deadline, then that was not your fault.

If our perceptions are valid, then a therapist can help us evaluate them in a healthy and non-destructive manner. They can help us solve any problems and learn to accept ourselves and our difficulties.

The thoughts that pop into our minds are automatic and can greatly affect how we feel. But by going through this questioning process, we are able to analyze the situation, our perspectives, and our feelings. This will allow us to overcome our own insecurities, react to situations in a healthier manner, and live happier lives.

The Connection between Our Situations and Our Thoughts

Mary had been at a loss. Lately, she was having trouble sleeping between insomnia keeping her up for hours on end, only to be woken up by nightmares. During the day, she was feeling listless. While she wanted to do more than sit around, she couldn't bring herself to put energy into anything. She had even lost interest in eating and was no longer staying in contact with friends.

Worried about Mary, after a month of prodding her older sister, Angela, had finally been able to convince her to go see a psychologist. While Mary knew on some level that there was nothing wrong with seeing a psychologist, she was also nervous. It was difficult to talk about how she was feeling and the thought of telling a stranger was scary. Not only that, but she didn't want to be stigmatized as a "crazy" person. She knew that all too often people with mental illnesses are treated poorly. But she didn't want her sister Angela to worry, so she had finally relented and agreed to go.

While going into therapy, Mary continued to feel nervous so she had Angela go in with her. She just wanted to get it done with and go back home.

The doctor noticed that while Angela was dressed nicely in a dress and her hair styled, Mary, on the other hand, had dressed in leggings and a wrinkled tunic and her hair looked like it hadn't been washed in a few days.

After talking with Mary for a little while, the doctor began to get to the root of what had been affecting her. After having a close friend and two pets all die of illness within the past year, Mary was feeling as if everyone she cared about was going to be taken away from her. She felt as though everyone she loved could die at any moment. When she couldn't get in contact with someone, she feared that they had died. Not only that, but she felt guilty. She was worried that she could have somehow done more to help her pets who had died of bacterial infections and cancer. She felt guilt over still being alive when her friend was dead.

During the appointment, she couldn't hold in the tears but her sister and the doctor were there for her all the while. By the end of the appointment, Mary wasn't better but a little of the weight had been lifted off of her shoulders after voicing her pain. She had also been diagnosed with depression due to her loss of appetite, fatigue, insomnia, loss of interest, guilt, and a general feeling of sadness. Having a name for what she was experiencing gave her hope especially because the doctor encouraged her that they could help her. Mary set up three follow up appointments.

The five-part cognitive model for Mary is as follows:

Environment/Situation: The death of a friend and pets.

Physical Reaction: loss of appetite, insomnia, fatigue.

Moods: Depressed

Behaviors/Reaction: Difficulty accomplishing tasks, avoiding friends and family.

Thoughts: *"It's my fault," "Everyone is going to die and leave me behind," "I could have done something differently," "What's even the point of living?"*

We will explore Mary's story more soon, but first, let's look at some other people who may benefit from cognitive behavioral therapy.

Lydia was recently promoted. This promotion had required her to move out of state, but she was closer to her family and childhood friends. She could not have been more excited about this change in her life and career! But within a few weeks of moving into her new apartment, someone else moved in next door. This person had a dog. Not just a dog though, this dog was large and it would run around next door banging against the floor and walls. When she passed it in the halls, then it would pull at the leash trying to smell everything, including Lydia.

The life she had dreamed of was soon becoming a nightmare. Lydia would wake up to nightmares sweating and struggling to catch her breath. She dreaded leaving her apartment for fear that she would run across either her neighbor's dog or another person's dog. She found herself staying at home whenever she could manage. One day when she had to go shopping, Lydia ended up with her heart racing, lungs struggling, extreme sweating, and jumping at the slightest sound. It was so scary. She thought she was having a heart attack. But after a long trip to the ER, the doctors found that there was nothing physically wrong with her. She was at a loss as to what to do.

And then, when she was talking to one of her childhood friends on the phone to avoid having to leave the house, they mentioned cognitive behavioral therapy. Lydia was willing to try anything. She didn't want to let this ruin her career, or much worse, her life.

After looking online for psychologists in the area, Lydia called one nearby. She questioned the doctor endlessly on cognitive behavioral therapy to be sure that they were well versed in it. Not only that, but she wanted to know if the doctor believed it could help her. The doctor assured her that they could at the very least make things a bit easier for Lydia, so she set an appointment.

At the appointment, the doctor uncovered why Lydia's anxiety suddenly got worse. Not only did she have a sudden life change and have a large active dog living next door, but the previous year she also went through a difficult divorce. Lydia never would have connected the two, but the stress of the past year had been weighing on her more than she realized. While she was proud of herself for the promotion, she was also holding herself to the unrealistic standards and stressing over appearing perfect among her peers in her profession.

All of this stress together led to Lydia developing an anxiety disorder which was manifesting largely by a fear of dogs due to childhood trauma. In order to address these issues, the doctor helped Lydia uncover her five-point cognitive model also known as the ABC model.

Environment/Situation: Large dog living next door, promotion, a recent move, recent divorce, and childhood trauma to dogs.

Physical Reaction: Cold sweats, difficulty breathing, racing heart rate, jumpy reactions.

Moods: Fearful, stressed, panic

Behaviors/Reaction: Avoiding tasks, considering moving but unable to get out of the contract for her apartment.

Thoughts: *"Something terrible will happen if I see a dog," "I'm having a heart attack," "I'm dying,"* or *"What if I see a dog and fall to pieces?"*

As it is plain to see, the cognitive model works for both depression and anxiety, as well as other disorders or even mentally healthy people. Whereas people with depression such as Mary often experience a slowing down, people like Lydia who has anxiety often notice a speeding up.

You see this in Mary when she wants to do nothing all day, loses her appetite, and is fatigued. On the other hand, Lydia experienced a racing heart rate, increased sweating, and she was jumpy. While depressed thoughts often center on a past set of events, anxious thoughts often center on the present and future.

Before we look at how Mary and Lydia were helped by cognitive behavioral therapy, let's look at Matt's story.

Matt was not the type of person to go to therapy. Not that there is anything wrong with therapy, but he grew up in a family who never talked about their problems. He was raised to believe that "real men" don't go to therapy. But Matt had overcome these feelings and was sitting in the office of a local psychologist anyway.

Why? Well, Matt had come to his breaking point and realized that he couldn't live the way he had been for the past several years any longer. This is because Matt struggled with alcoholism and his temper. When life got too stressful, he felt saddened or pressured, or when he began to think of all the ways in which he felt like a failure, he would drink. Only when he drank would he feel free from all of his negative thoughts. He knew drinking only worsened things in the long-run, especially when he drove while under the influence, but he felt that he couldn't give it up.

This drinking would get in the way of his work. He would pull himself up in the mornings and barely feel up to showering with his pounding headache from the previous night. This left him constantly stressed that he was going to be fired. Despite his excellent performance reviews, he was always in fear that when his boss spoke to him or when the phone rang, he was going to be fired.

Just as bad as his drinking was his temper which would come out whenever someone pointed out his flaws or when he felt either slighted or inferior. While he never hit a person, his words and the volume he said at them did quite a bit of damage. This is how Matt ended up seeing the psychologist.

Because after dating the girl of his dreams for two years and living with her for a year now, she broke up with Matt. He let his anger get the best of him and ended up yelling at her and saying some things that couldn't be forgiven or forgotten. After she left, Matt drank so much that he ended up in the hospital.

Matt was raised in a family where perfection is everything. His parents grew him up on the saying, *"if you can't do it right then don't do it at all."* While they may have shown him love, he always felt as if he was a disappointment compared to his brother who was a star on the football field and a straight-A student. Even when Matt was able to perfectly hit a curveball and steal two bases in a high school baseball game, he felt as though he had failed because another kid on his team had hit more balls than him. Even if he was successful, it wasn't good enough unless he was the best.

When Matt first sat down in front of the psychologist and she asked him what he hoped to get out of their appointments, he laughed and said, *"I want you to make me perfect."* The psychologist smiled but she said, *"Why don't we try helping you learn to be happy with who you are instead?"*

Matt gulped at this but gave a slight nod.

After their first session, the doctor was able to create a cognitive model of Matt.

Environment/Situation: Lifelong pressure by both his parents and himself to attain perfection, alcoholism.

Physical Reaction: Difficulty sleeping, stomach pains.

Moods: Angry, nervous, stressed, and depressed.

Behaviors/Reaction: Attempts to uphold perfection, binge drinking, anger outburst.

Thoughts: *"I'm not good enough," "I'm going to be fired," "Something awful is going to happen," "If someone criticizes me, then they are slighting me," "Drinking will help me feel better,"* and *"I'm a failure."*

While these three cases may be different, Matt shares some similarities with both Lydia and Mary. Matt's self-deprecating viewpoint and negativity are due to depression, which Mary also has. And his constant worry paired with his need to be perfect is anxiety, which Lydia also has.

Mediating Our Reactions

When Mary first began to pull herself away from her loved ones, her sister Angela suspected it was part of the normal grieving process. Especially since Mary had lost so much in such a short time. But when it continued for month after month, Angela began to worry. When she would ask Mary about it, she would get vague answers such as "I just don't feel like doing much" and "What's the point." This didn't sound like the Mary that Angela had known her whole life.

But after speaking with the psychologist, they were able to uncover why Mary was withdrawing. Due to losing her friend and beloved pets, Mary was trying to protect herself. Since she was feeling like anyone else could die and be taken away from her, she was subconsciously retreating. This means that she wasn't even aware of the reasons she was doing it, she just knew it was too difficult to remain social.

Here's the thing, our thoughts and behaviors are not usually separated. If we think and feel one way, it will usually affect our behaviors. If we are utilizing self-control, then it may not show very much, but some people may still pick up on it.

For instance, if you are trying to act friendly to some relatives you hate being around. You could be exceedingly kind and charming, but it would probably show in small subtle ways that you were uncomfortable. Occasionally, it may leak out through your tone of voice, word choices, or body language.

This works the other way around too. If we believe we are able to accomplish something, then we are more likely to succeed. This doesn't mean that the power of belief is all powerful. We first have to put in the work to succeed.

One shining example of this is the famed Russian weightlifter, Vasily Alekseyev. Back in 1970, no professional weightlifter had ever been able to lift five-hundred pounds above their head. Despite holding the weightlifting world record, Alekseyev had never been able to attain the five-hundred-pound goal. Then when Alekseyev was preparing for an important competition, his personal trainer told him that he would be lifting a weight which he was well familiar with lifting.

Alekseyev successfully lifted the weight and only realized after the fact that his trainer had deceived him. He now holds the new world record for lifting a total of five-hundred pounds above his head.

By deceiving him, Alekseyev's trainer had been able to relieve him of the mindset that told him he couldn't attain his goal. Not only that, but once Alekseyev learned that he could attain five-hundred pounds, he went on to lift over five-hundred and sixty pounds overhead!

This is a wonderful example of how our beliefs impact our actions and chances of success. Because this is not some story of the power of belief impossibly removing a person's boundaries. Instead, Alekseyev worked long and hard for years to attain his goal. It was his hard work combined with the belief of his success that enabled him to succeed. The two working belief in hard work and belief in yourself working in tandem can help you overcome your hurdles.

Just like Alekseyev's thoughts influenced his behavior, we all have thoughts that influence us on a day to day basis. If it is a holiday and your family is gathered around a feast, there could be many possible thoughts that would influence your behavior. Some thoughts that might influence your behavior include:

- *"There are only two seats left at the table. I don't want to sit next to my racist Uncle Joe, but the other seat is more difficult to get to."*

- *"I'm really stuffed, I shouldn't eat more. But if I wait, we might run out of my favorite pecan pie."*

- *"I'm so tired of hearing my Aunt Jackie Anne talk down to me. But I don't want to cause a fight on a holiday."*

- *"It's getting late, I really should go home. But I'm having such a good conversation with my cousin Alex, I don't want to leave."*

All of these thoughts and more may only quickly pass through your mind. Yet, they can influence your behavior without your realization. Sometimes, you may be completely unaware of these automatic passing thoughts like Mary. While Mary didn't realize why she was pulling herself away from her loved ones, it was impacting her behavior. These thoughts can run through our minds so quickly that we are not fully aware of them. All the same, we can respond to the thoughts out of habit.

Previously, Mary was unable to explain why she was withdrawing from all the people and animals she cared about. Thankfully, cognitive behavioral therapy was able to help Mary recognize her thought processes and how they impacted her actions. She learned to acknowledge the thoughts she was having, even those that were just passing. Such as *"I'm going to lose everyone anyways, I don't want to get hurt again," "what's the point of having pets when they are just going to die,"* and *"I won't enjoy myself if I do this activity, why bother?"*

Likewise, Lydia learned to identify the thoughts that were impacting her actions. She learned that thoughts such as *"something terrible will happen," "what if," "I'm going to fail,"* and *"I'm weak"* were all contributing to her fear. The divorce, recent move, promotion, and childhood dog trauma contributed to her anxiety. But it was her thoughts that were controlling her actions and thereby worsening the anxiety.

Matt learned that while he is responsible for his own actions such as drinking and anger, that his troubling thought process is a result from how he grew up. By identifying what these troubling thought processes are, his psychologist helped him learn to overcome them. Thoughts such as *"I'm not good enough," "I'm going to be fired," "something awful is going to happen," "If someone criticizes me, then they are slighting me," "drinking will help me feel better,"* and *"I'm a failure"* were only getting in his way. These thoughts had previously been subconscious passing thoughts that he didn't even recognize. But as he began to act on them, they developed into bad habits which he had a difficult time resisting. The first step of purging these thoughts and actions from his life was by identifying them.

Whether you have anxiety, depression, alcoholism, anger management difficulties, ADHD, control issues, or a number of other issues, the use of cognitive behavioral therapy can help. In fact, CBT can even help people who are mentally healthy and doing well in their lives. This is because the use of CBT can help make us more aware of our thoughts, preventing us from developing mentally unhealthy thought processes, and helping us to reach our goals.

One example of cognitive behavioral therapy helping in daily life is with weight loss. While we often think of weight loss in terms of what we eat in carbs, fat, and protein, there is more to it than that. This is obvious when you see that obesity is raging across America and has become a national problem. While what we eat is important, our habits and lifestyle are large factors as well. We have to learn new behaviors and habits if we hope to stick to a healthy diet and exercise routine.

Yet, learning these new behaviors isn't easy. If it were simple, then it wouldn't be the problem it is in modern society. The use of cognitive behavioral therapy has been shown to help us change the way in which we react to circumstances and our own thoughts. The techniques that teach these have many daily applications including leading us toward our goals such as weight loss.

By using CBT, you can learn to set specific goals around your eating and lifestyle such as choosing to replace sugar with stevia leaf extract. You will learn that these specific goals rather than general goals like *"I want to eat healthier"* will help you better stick to your diet and stay motivated.

Rather than beating yourself up if you don't reach a goal, you will learn to deal with it in a healthy manner. You can self-monitor to identify your challenges and barriers and change your behavior to overcome them. Many people will often stay motivated to lose weight by thinking negatively of ourselves. This can lead to feelings of defeat and negative choices. By learning to accept ourselves and overcome our barriers we can attain physical health while remaining mentally healthy.

By setting goals, an important aspect of cognitive behavioral therapy, we can better increase our chances of success. Not only because we can only attain goals if we know what those goals are, but because they will boost our confidence. If we set small goals, then after achieving them we will see that we can attain them. This helps to push back against negative thoughts such as *"I can't do this"* and *"I'm a failure."* Over time, this will boost our self-confidence and our perception of ourselves. We will be less inclined to negative trails of thought.

Adopting a healthier lifestyle, both physically and mentally, isn't easy. But with the help of cognitive behavioral therapy, you can become more confident, less anxious, and reach your goals whether they are to lose weight or simply to live happily.

An Overview of Cognitive Behavioral Therapy Principles

There are many tools you can use in CBT. They may seem simple, but if you use all of them together with a genuine effort, then you will find that you can have a powerful change within yourself. The effectiveness of cognitive behavioral therapy is used internationally to help people suffering from everything from post-traumatic stress disorder to social anxiety disorder. Following, we will explore the main principles of cognitive behavioral therapy. If you implement these into your life, then you are sure to experience benefits.

Counteract Negative Thought Patterns

If you find yourself having negative thoughts, then examine them more closely rather than allowing them to fester in your mind. Look for evidence against your negative thoughts. If you are experiencing feelings of worthlessness, you can find ways in which you have value and worth to prove the negative thoughts as false. In a notebook, write down the evidence as to why the negative thought is wrong and then you can write out a more balanced thought. Such as "I have worth because (fill in the blank)."

When people are depressed they will often hold back or dampen any positive thoughts regarding themselves or their life in general. Even if some part of them knows that they aren't worthless, they refuse to acknowledge this. By refuting the negative thoughts and replacing it with positive thoughts, a person can begin to change their entire thought process and cognition.

Journal, Mind Map, and Brainstorm

Writing a journal can be extremely productive in changing our cognition. This is because when we get the positive ideas out of our heads and put them on paper, we are more likely to believe and adopt them. If you are struggling with obstacles obstructing your progress, then you can mind map solution to those problems. To do this, in a journal write your obstacle or problem in the center of the page. Then as you consider solutions to the problem, you can write them out from the center so that it resembles a spider web. Don't worry about how plausible the solutions are at this time. Let your mind roam freely. After you have multiple solutions written out, you can analyze which ones are the best fits for you or if you need to adapt them slightly.

Analyze Your Feelings and Thoughts

If you are having a difficult time overcoming binge eating, then conduct experiments on your thoughts and analyze the results. If you are thinking negative thoughts such as *"I'll binge less if I chastise or punish myself,"* think of a more positive attitude. For example, *"I'll eat less junk food and forgive myself if I binge eat."* You can write down both thought processes and then try them both out. If you binge eat after the negative thought or the positive thought, write down the results. How much did you binge eat? Knowing this can give you objective data on what can help you overcome your obstacles.

Problem Solving

Psychologists will help addicts with cognitive behavioral therapy by creating new healthy coping mechanisms. They do this by first assessing what problems that their patients run into that lead them to drink, using drugs, self-harming, or other behaviors. They can then create strategies to deal with these problems and urges which give the patient confidence and helps them take control over their addiction.

Visualize Daily

Positive thinking greatly impacts our mental state, long-term thought process, and even our success. Every morning, one of the first things you do should be to imagine your day going well. Even if you have an overwhelming schedule, remind yourself that you can do it. Imagine successfully getting everything done well and having a happy productive day. You can do this while you lay in bed, brush your teeth, apply makeup, or whatever. But do it early in the morning as one of your first tasks.

In the evenings, visualize over your day. Remember any success or positive events. If anything didn't go well, then imagine it as if it had gone well. Forgive yourself of any mistakes and use it as a learning experience. Rather than being filled with negative thoughts of failure before bed, let yourself enjoy your success and joy.

Doing this will not only lessen insomnia, over time it can help you sleep more soundly, lessen bad dreams, and even promote a more healthy cognition overall.

Think Positive

You will often hear people who are successful either in business or life touts the benefits of positive thinking. These people never let what others may consider failure to hold them back. There are countless stories of people picking themselves up by the bootstraps and working hard. They overcome hurdle after hurdle and they get to where they want to be. Whether that goal is to be overcome addiction, become financially stable, get out of debt, or to become rich, positive thinking paired with hard work can get you there.

Sure, positive thinking on its own can't do anything. You have to put the work in. But the two working together can do amazing things. You can never succeed when you let every obstacle or failure overcome you. Rather, you need to learn to overcome the obstacles and seeming failure.

Every day, look for opportunities to change the way you think about and respond to obstacles. This can be in the little things. For instance, instead of thinking *"the weather is terrible,"* consider five positive aspects of rain. It waters the grass, helps the flowers grow, freshens the air, your roof isn't leaking, and it washes away the dirt and grime.

Set a timer on your phone so that you don't forget. At least twice a day, practice thinking of positives regarding the situation you are in. Learning to think positively about the seemingly little things in life will make it easier and more natural to think positively about the more difficult aspects.

Plan Fun Activities

Even if you are extremely busy, schedule a little time every day for a fun positive activity. This can be something simple as relaxing for ten minutes while you listen to a few favorite songs, taking a bubble bath, sketching, or reading. It doesn't have to take long, but ten simple minutes of doing a positive and enjoyable activity can do wonders for your mental health.

By taking an enjoyable break, you can recharge your mind and body and have something to look forward to. Doing this can help to interrupt negative thoughts and help you learn to relax and enjoy yourself again.

Write down a list of enjoyable, positive, and healthy activities that you can do. Some of them may only take ten minutes while others may take an hour, it is up to you. Every day, include one of these activities to help build a positive thought process in your brain and relieve stress.

Disappointment is Normal

We will all experience disappointments in life. Whether that disappointment is that the rain caused your plans to be canceled or you didn't get accepted into your college of choice, we can shape how this disappointment affects us.

Learn to forgive yourself and cut yourself a little slack. The way in which we react to both the ups and downs in our lives will shape our joy and future. If we are unable to get past what we perceive as a failure, then we will continue to live in a vicious cycle of negativity and regret.

Allow yourself to feel the disappointment, but then learn to accept it and look at it objectively. It is important to be able to distinguish which disappointments were caused by either our own actions or situations out of our control.

If it was something out of our control, then we need to let go of the negativity. If the disappointment is a result of your own actions, then you can learn to improve or change your behavior. Learn from your mistakes, forgive yourself, and then move forward.

Mary, Lydia, and Matt have learned the basics of what cognitive behavioral therapy or CBT entails. They now know that it's important to recognize their passing thoughts. Yet, they still have much to learn. Continue reading to learn how these three people are able to progress and take control of their lives.

Chapter 2: The Mind with Cognitive Behavioral Therapy

In the previous chapter, you learned an overview summary of behavioral cognitive therapy. This includes practices such as analyzing your feelings, positive thinking, spending time doing activities you enjoy, and more. But to successfully utilize CBT, you need to know more. In this chapter, we will dig deeper into the practices of CBT and how you can benefit from them.

Firstly, it's important to understand how your brain responds to cognitive behavioral therapy. There have been some amazing studies on the matter. Not only does CBT affect your mind and the way you think, but it can also even affect how your brain operates as a biological function.

A group of researchers from universities in Sweden such as Linköping University decided to get together and study cognitive behavioral therapy. They did this because we have long known that the brain is incredibly adaptable. Some studies have even shown that activities such as video games and juggling can affect the volume of your brain.

To study how CBT affects the brain, the researchers conducted a study on a group of people by having them participate in cognitive behavioral therapy through the internet. One of the most common mental illnesses was the focus of this study. This illness is social anxiety disorder and affects an estimated fifteen million people within America.

Magnetic resonance imaging, commonly referred to as MRI, was conducted on all the participants both at the beginning and end of their CBT treatment. This study is amazing because not only do we have studies proving the mental effects of CBT, but this one is even looking at the biological effects.

In the initial brain scans, it was found that people with social anxiety disorder have an altered brain volume and the activity in a portion of their brain is increased. This portion of the brain is the amygdala, which is used primarily to make decisions, process memories, and emotional responses. It's easy to imagine how these changes could affect our mental state.

It may seem as if this biological function is out of our control, but this study proves otherwise. In fact, the study found that when the participants with social anxiety disorder completed nine weeks of CBT through the internet, their brains improved. These people experienced a reduction in brain volume and a decrease in the activity of the amygdala. The patients whose anxiety improved the most also experienced the greatest decrease in brain volume and amygdala activity.

This study proves the power of cognitive behavioral therapy. It isn't simply a false sense of positive thinking that some people may assume. Rather, it creates a real change in how you perceive the world, your reactions, your mood, and yes, even your brain.

What about people like Mary who suffers from debilitating depression? I have good news. Cognitive behavioral therapy has had great success on people living with depression. The results are amazing. CBT has been shown to be twice as effective as antidepressants in preventing depressive relapses.

The study which proved this was hoping to find the effects of both antidepressants and CBT on depressed people. While the researchers hypothesized that both treatments would treat depression similarly, they were surprised by the results.

Throughout treatment with some participants on antidepressants and others practicing cognitive behavioral therapy, the researchers would scan their brains with an MRI.

They were soon surprised to find that antidepressants and CBT impact completely different areas of the brain for people with depression. Antidepressants would reduce the activity in the emotional center of the brain known as the limbic system. Surprisingly, CBT helped to calm the area of the brain which is responsible for our reasoning, the cortex.

This means that while antidepressants reduce our emotions, CBT can actively help us to process them in a more proactive and healthy manner. This explains why CBT is much more effective in the long run and less likely to result in a depressive relapse down the road.

Post-traumatic stress disorder, often simply referred to as PTSD is a common condition which people suffer from after undergoing a traumatic event. Most people only consider veterans who went to war having PTSD. However, there are many other people who live every day with this condition. For instance, people who have undergone painful surgeries, those who have been in accidents, people who have lost someone close to them, and sexual assault victims. The symptoms of PTSD vary from person to person, but a few of the symptoms include:

- Flashbacks reliving a traumatic experience.
- Nightmares.

- Avoiding events, places, or objects that remind a person of the traumatic experience.

- Feeling tense, on edge, and easily startled.

- Experiencing angry outbursts.

- Having difficulty sleeping.

- Difficulty remembering or recalling the traumatic event.

- Guilt, blame, or other negative thoughts towards yourself.

- Loss of interest in your daily life and enjoyable activities.

There is much more, but these are some of the most common symptoms of PTSD. If you suspect you may have PTSD, please talk with a psychologist or psychiatrist and they can walk you through it. It is always recommended to get help from a trained professional who can personalize your care and treatment plan. However, this book can help alongside your doctor during your journey towards healing.

One study showing the effects of cognitive behavioral therapy was conducted with the participation of one-hundred children who were suffering from PTSD after being sexually assaulted. They had the children go into therapy, some with their mothers present and others with solely the therapist. Their condition was checked at regular intervals to see how the children were healing from the trauma.

The children completed tests both before, during, and after the treatment periods. After the original cognitive behavioral therapy, the children's tests scores improved significantly. These continued to improve over the following two years. This suggests that CBT is a successful treatment option for long-term improvement and care.

But in order to receive these benefits, it is important to understand in-depth how to utilize cognitive behavioral therapy. This therapy is a powerful tool and if you understand its basis and how to follow it through, you can experience amazing benefits.

While cognitive behavioral therapy involves some positive thinking, there is more to it than that. In fact, if you tell a person who is depressed, anxious, stressed, or suffering from trauma simply "just think positively," it will only cause them further stress. This is because positive thoughts alone are not enough to cause lasting change. When a person tries this and it doesn't work, they are likely to feel frustrated. This down-spiral further increases negative thoughts.

Instead, it is important to practice using your mind as a tool over your mood. This will help you to consider all the information you have access to from various angles. If you are able to consider a situation (whether negative or positive) from all sides, then you can find a new understanding and solutions to your problems.

A good example of this is Lydia. If she simply told herself "I won't have anxiety when I see the neighbor's dog. I'm perfectly fine," she would be unrealistic and wouldn't be prepared for the anxiety she is likely to face once she sees the dog. Once she begins to feel anxiety upon seeing the dog, Lydia may end up feeling like a failure. Even a small amount of anxiety will make her feel as if there is no point to positive thinking.

Instead, Lydia will do better if she studies the situation from all sides and then decides on a solution for how to react if she becomes anxious. She can then think positively trusting in herself and her plan to help get her through coming across dogs. This is more successful because if we only allow false positive thoughts, then we will be unprepared for difficult situations.

Identifying your thoughts and then analyzing, testing, considering alternatives, and using your mind over your mood are important aspects of CBT. Although it is equally important to make behavioral changes along with these, it is important to keep in mind that cognitive behavioral therapy is consists of many components. Just like the inner pieces of a clock, CBT is only successful when all of the parts are working together.

Work on identifying your thoughts and analyzing them, thinking more positively, coming up with plans to reduce anxiety, and more. But also makes changes in your life. These changes will vary from person to person.

Rather than avoiding all dogs, Lydia could try acclimating to friendly small dogs until she feels comfortable. This will help her overcome her fear overtime and learn how to better manage her anxiety.

Mary needs to make a point of communicating with friends and spending time doing enjoyable activities. Her depression may make her feel like doing nothing but lying in bed and staring at the ceiling. But in order to improve the depression, she needs to get back out into life.

With Matt's alcoholism, he shouldn't keep alcohol around the house or go to bars. Instead, he needs to make a goal of becoming sober and attend regular meetings for alcoholics.

Likewise, if someone is being abused, they

shouldn't simply "think happy thoughts" and become more submissive to their oppressor. Instead, their focus should be on finding a safe way to escape the abusive situation.

Now that you understand that this process is not solely about a false and short lasting positive thinking, it is time to address our negative thought processes. These thoughts control our actions in many ways. Maybe you were too scared to follow the career of your dreams because you might fail. Perhaps you become so overwhelmed that you procrastinate constantly. Or maybe you begin binge eating because you ate a single cookie and feel like a failure so what even is the point? All of these negative thoughts and more are damaging. Over time, they not only prevent us from attaining our goals and the life we desire, but they also will increasingly affect our mental health.

This is because of our negative thoughts and circumstances will accumulate. This shows in Lydia's story, where her trauma of dogs didn't surface until after she had been through a stressful divorce, move, and promotion. After all of the negative thoughts and emotions of the past year accumulated, she was unable to handle the anxiety and it manifested by bringing back her childhood trauma.

These thoughts can also combine in ways that make us think more negatively of ourselves such as in Matt's case, or as if there is no point in doing anything, like with Mary.

It is important to recognize all of your negative thoughts and learn to analyze and test them and then overcome them. But to do that, first, you need to know how to recognize them. There are ten main types of negative thoughts. Many people will experience most, if not all of these from time to time. But people often fall into centering on one or two types of negative thoughts.

These include:

1. Focusing on the Negative: *"Everything always goes wrong, life is just one disappointment after another."*

2. Negative Labeling of Yourself: *"I'm a terrible person and a failure. If people knew who I really was, they would leave me."*

3. Perfectionism: *"I have to do everything perfectly, otherwise I am a failure. I can't let anyone see anything of mine unless it's perfect."*

4. Constant Approval Needed: *"I have to make everyone like me. That's the only way I can be happy."*

5. Worst Case Scenario: *"Everything is going to be a disaster. It can't go well. I'm doomed."*

6. Ignoring the Present: *"I'll take care of myself later. For now, I have a list of things to accomplish."*

7. Other People Should Do What I Think: *"My friend shouldn't be posting so many photos of her boyfriend on social media. My adult daughter shouldn't be pursuing that career. That stranger shouldn't be wearing that, it's unflattering."*

8. Mind Reader: *"Other people must hate me, otherwise they wouldn't behave that way."*

9. Living in the Past: *"I'm miserable. I'm going to lay here and think about what happened to make me feel this way."*

10. Glass Half Empty: *"I don't trust people who are happy. If anything good ever happens in my life, then it is all going to be destroyed."*

The thoughts will vary from person to person depending on their situation. But most people will fit into at least one or two of these categories. After we figure out how we think, we can begin to counteract it. To do this, we start by finding the deceptions within those thought patterns.

Keep a little notebook with you or simply use a smartphone and keep track of your negative thoughts. You want a list that resembles sections titled:

- Situation

- Mood

- Automatic Thoughts or Images

- Evidence that Supports my Thoughts

- Evidence that Disproves my Thoughts

- Alternative Healthy Thoughts

- New Mood

When creating this list, you should use the four W's to help you. This means always fill out who, what, when, and where. You want to be specific, because if you simply state that it was happening "all day," then you are unable to target the cause behind the feelings. But if you know that you felt this way at 8:30 am when you were on your way to work, this narrows things down greatly.

Under the mood column, write any and all of the moods you were feeling at the time. You may have been feeling overwhelmed, depressed, anxious, sad, hurt, nervous, angry, or other emotions. When listing these, it is beneficial to rate them on a score of zero to one-hundred.

These allow people who experience panic or anxiety attacks to log the severity.

Under the automatic thoughts or images, write any of the thoughts that were going through your head at the time. Taking the example from a moment ago, imagine that the thoughts running through your mind on the way to work that triggered this were *"I'm going to be late," "They'll fire me and then I won't have a job,"* and *"I'm worthless"*. If these thoughts were running through your head, you would write them down in this column and then analyze them in the following columns.

Next, tie together the columns for automatic thoughts and mood together on a rating of zero to one-hundred. For each thought, rate how it made you feel. Did the thought of being late makes you twenty percent anxious? The thought of being fired and without a job eighty percent scared? The thought of being worthless ninety percent depressed? By ranking the emotions tied to each of these thoughts, you can learn to better recognize damaging thoughts and proceed to overcome them.

The following step is one of the most important in this method and that is analyzing the evidence on whether or not your feelings are true or false. This can help us learn to identify what is a fact rather than our interpretation of a situation. There are many questions you can ask yourself to analyze these thoughts, but in the example we have been exploring, you might ask "Do I know I won't make it to work on time," "Are they likely to fire someone for being late once," "am I blaming myself for something out of my control," "When I'm not feeling this way, what do I think of this situation," "Are there any positives about myself that I am ignoring", and "If my best friend knew how I was feeling, what would they say?"

After analyzing the thought, you can fill in the alternative healthy thought section. Here, if you found that your thoughts weren't true, then you could fill in a more accurate thought. This might be "I haven't been late this year and my boss loves me, they are unlikely to fire me. I know I'm not worthless, every person has value and I have learned to be kind and compassionate. I am a valuable person"

If your thoughts were partially true, take the new information to write a more balanced view. For instance "my boss won't be happy, but I doubt I will be without a job. I may have slept through my alarm this morning, but that doesn't negate my intrinsic worth as a human being. I can take steps to wake up on time in the future."

After you analyze your thoughts and create new

healthier and more balanced thoughts, you can rate how the new thoughts make you feel on a level of zero to one-hundred like you did with the original thought.

While this forum will change moment by moment for any given person, depending on the situations they are going through, let's look at what it might look like if Mary and Matt filled out this forum.

Mary:

- **Situation:**
  Didn't answer the phone when a friend called at noon.

- **Mood:**
  Depressed ninety percent, anxious thirty percent, worthlessness fifty percent.

- **Automatic Thoughts or Images:**
  "I can't be close to people. If I am, they'll die and I'll lose them," "I'm bad luck to have around," "Why am I even alive?"

- **Evidence that Supports my Thoughts:**
  My loved ones keep dying.

- **Evidence that Disproves my Thoughts:**
  Death is a part of life.
  My friends and pets were ill.

I cared for them as best as I could do while they were alive.
Their deaths were out of my hands.
People aren't bad or good luck.
Everyone is alive for a purpose.
My friends care about me and want me around.

- **Alternative Healthy Thoughts:** *"I'm sad that they died, but it wasn't my fault and I can't blame myself. My friends care about me and if I wasn't around, they would be sad."*

- **New Mood:**
  Depressed forty percent, sad twenty percent, hopeful twenty percent.

As you can see, Mary may not feel all better, but she is working through her emotions. Her thoughts and mood are more stable now and she is reminded of why she is alive.

Now, let's look at Matt:

- **Situation:**
  His ex-girlfriend came by for a box of her stuff at 6 pm.

- **Mood:**
  Angry eighty percent, sad fifty percent.

- **Automatic Thoughts or Images:**
  "Why did she have to come by tonight when I was already having a bad day? She should have known it was too soon to see each other, now I miss her even more. This is her fault. If she had only forgiven me. I want a drink."

- **Evidence that Supports my Thoughts:**
  I apologized, she could have forgiven me.

- **Evidence that Disproves my Thoughts:**
  She needed her stuff and had a right to come get it.
  Even after the breakup, she was being kind and asked how I was doing.
  The breakup isn't her fault. She stuck with me for two years despite my drinking and anger.
  She doesn't have to forgive me and even if she has, that doesn't mean she is required to stay with me.

- **Alternative Healthy Thoughts:**
  "I'm sad that we broke up, but I hope she lives a happy life. Now that I am single, I can focus on bettering my own life, becoming sober, and controlling my temper. This is better for both of us in the long-run. A drink won't help me and I want to stay sober."

- **New Mood:**
  Sad fifteen percent, encouraged twenty percent, motivated fifty percent.

While Matt began the process as angry, as he worked through his feelings, whether they were true or false and developed a healthier alternative thought, he was able to work through his anger. This helped him to accept the breakup at the moment and encouraged him to stay sober. He may struggle with his anger and the breakup from time to time in the future, but if he continues to get through it in this healthy manner, then he can improve his life, learn to control his anger, and resist alcohol. Over time, the breakup will begin to hurt less.

It is important to retain awareness of your own mental state. To do this, try to fill out this forum regularly, especially whenever you notice your mood is low or your thoughts are destructive. But sometimes it can be hard to start because we are greatly lacking an awareness of our thoughts. This can be especially true when we have been living with a condition such as depression or anxiety for a long time. We become so accustomed to it that it turns into background noise. We need to learn to listen into this background noise so that we can tune it into a beautiful melody rather than a high-pitched static. Asking different questions based on our moods can help.

Generalized questions are a good place to start because you can ask them of yourself, no matter what your mood is. You may find it difficult to place a finger on exactly what you had been thinking of prior to a mood shift, but with some time, you will become an expert at realizing and recalling what is impacting your mood. After practice, many people will be able to place their finger on what upset them simply by answering these two questions:

- What was the last thing going through my mind before I noticed my mood shift?

- What memories or images was I experiencing?

The second question is regarding images and memories because many people find that their strongest mood shifts aren't a response to a specific thought. Rather, it was a response to a memory or image they thought of. For instance, for a split second, someone could remember a still image of a loved one in the hospital. If you have a lot going on in your life, it is easy to get distracted and not remember what triggered it, but the negative emotions remain. This is why it's important to learn to target and analyze what is affecting you.

After answering the generalized questions, you can answer some more specific mood-related questions.

When people are anxious, they often consider worst-case scenarios of what could happen in the near or distant future. We overestimate what could go wrong while simultaneously underestimating ourselves. When you find yourself anxious, scared, or nervous, then ask yourself *"what am I afraid might happen?"* and *"what is the worst that could happen?"*

If you find yourself depressed, it is easy to be self-critical or even hate yourself completely. In this case, it's easy to not just be critical about ourselves, but life in general as well. Therefore, if you are feeling depressed, sad, discouraged, or disappointed, I want you to ask yourself three questions. *"What does this mean about me?"*, *"What does this mean about my future?"*, and *"What does this mean about life?"*

People often feel guilt or shame in conjunction with their actions even if they didn't do anything wrong. For instance, people can have survivor's guilt if someone close to them died yet they survived. There was nothing wrong with them surviving and they couldn't have saved the other person, yet they feel guilty. Though these feelings can, of course, have validity as well. If you got into a fight with your sibling, you could feel guilty for something you said. If you find yourself feeling this way, ask yourself *"Did I hurt someone, break a law/rule, not have done something I should have, or otherwise gone against my moral code?", "What does this mean about how others feel about me?", "What do I think or believe about myself?",* and *"What would other people think if they knew?"*

We can often feel angry, irritated, or resentful if we have felt as if someone has harmed us in some way. Even if the person wasn't unjust or mistreating us, we can often feel antsy from anger. It is important to distinguish whether or not this anger is justified. There is righteous anger. For instance, we can be angry when we learn of a child being abused. Non-righteous anger would be us getting angry that the cheeseburger that we ordered had pickles when we asked for no pickles. Sure, the person who made the cheeseburger made a mistake, but it is not something to get upset about if they are willing to fix it for us. If you are having anger related feelings, ask yourself *"What does this mean about other people?"* and *"What does this mean about how other people feel about me?"*

By asking yourself these questions, you will learn to recognize your emotions and the thoughts, memories, and images that trigger them. While what other people do and say can impact our emotions, remember that it is ultimately how we respond to those people that impact our long-term emotional state.

Occasionally, you may want to try looking over some of the other questions that aren't in your emotional category. For instance, if you are feeling anxious, you still may benefit by asking yourself the depression questions. Over time, you may even develop some of your own questions which you find is helping you to identify why you are feeling or reacting in specific ways.

Chapter 3: Using Cognitive Behavioral Therapy in Daily Life

As children are growing up they are taught to think about what they might want to become when they grow up. Later on, they create career goals, learn about those careers, and are urged to choose a college major that applies to their field of choice. When applying to college, these now young adults spend lengths of time analyzing all of the benefits of their chosen college, but also of other colleges. Just in case, they are urged to send out letters to multiple colleges in case they don't get into their college of choice.

All of this is done because having goals is important. Without goals, we have no idea where we are going to end up or get there along the way. It may be fine to not have a goal when you are going on a stroll. But when it comes to your life and how you spend your years, you want to put a thought into it. If someone decides to work a retail job and spend their free time painting and growing plants, that is fine.

Someone else may have a goal of becoming a leading neurosurgeon. Neither goal is superior to the other. Simply, having a goal will help to motivate you and help you take steps to achieve your dream.

You picked up this book for a reason, what was it? Maybe a friend recommended it to you and you decided to give it a chance. But what within your heart made you decide to give it a chance? There is something in all of our lives that we feel dissatisfied with. Is your relationship with your parents strained? Do you have insomnia? Are you depressed? Do you find yourself relying on alcohol or drugs? Do you have a difficult time controlling your temper? If you can isolate the problems that led you to pick up this book, then you can more easily create meaningful goals.

To find your goals, try picking up a piece of paper and pen. Begin to write down goals as specific as you can. Goals such as "have less anxiety," "sleep better," "overcome my depression," and "create deeper relationships" are good.

Although to create great goals, you will want to be more specific. As you can see, the goals above can work for most anyone, so try to tailor your goals for you. This could mean you write "be around dogs without having anxiety attacks," "overcome the depression so that I can feel happy daily again," "reduce insomnia so that I can get seven hours of sleep every night," or "deepen my relationship with my parents so that I'm not stressed to be around them and we can easily chat."

With these more specific goals, you can have a better idea of how to attain them, as well as having the ability to track your progress.

After you write down your goals, write down the advantages of attaining them and the disadvantages of failing to attain them. This will help to motivate you further. It can also help you narrow down further goals that you might want to add to your goal list.

It is important to write this down, not just keep it as a mental list. There may not seem to be much of a difference, but the impacting of writing down your goal is huge. In fact, a professor at the Dominican University in California, Dr. Gail Matthews, recently studied this subject.

Dr. Matthews conducted this study on over two-hundred and sixty people. These people came from all around the world, different walks of lives, and a variety of careers. The results were astounding. While Dr. Matthews hypothesized that those who wrote down their goals would reach success at a higher rate, they did so at a remarkably higher level. The act of writing goals down is so significant, that people are forty-two percent more likely to achieve a goal if they write it down on a regular basis.

This statistic increases even further for people who share their goals with friends or family. Having someone who believes in you and your ability to succeed is powerful.

When creating goals, try to keep four aspects in mind. These will help your goals to be more powerful, helping you to measure your progress, stay encouraged, and eventually attain what you dream of.

Reflect on Your Life and Situation

We can only know where we want to be if we first know where we are currently at. Just like an ostrich is unable to see its surroundings and destination when it buries its head in the sand, we are unable to see where we want to end up if we are in denial of our life and mental health. Take some time with a pen and paper and honestly consider every aspect of your life. After considering different aspects, ask yourself if you are okay with that. If you aren't okay with portions of your life, then write them down.

You may need to take a week in order to honestly evaluate yourself and your goals and that is alright. It takes time to consider where we are at truthfully. See this as an opportunity for growth and improvement and get excited!

Know Your Dreams

In our modern society, most of us are constantly rushing. Whether we have jobs, family, sporting events, classes, kids, hobbies, or social lives to keep us busy, most of us find we have too few hours in the day. But humans also have an amazing ability to dream and create goals.

Honestly consider what these dreams and goals are. You may need to find some time to slow down in order to accomplish this. After all, you can't very well consider your dreams if you are being overwhelmed at work. If you give yourself some time to slow down and consider where you want to end up both in your future, in your daily life, and with your mental health, then you will better be able to make a plan. For instance, a future goal would be to graduate college in the major of your choice. A daily goal is to stay sober and avoid all alcohol. Mental health goals would be to have the ability to answer the phone without having an anxiety attack.

Create S.M.A.R.T Goals

An acronym common for creating strong goals. S.M.A.R.T goals are specific, measurable, attainable, realistic, and time-sensitive.

Stay Specific

Specific so that you know exactly where you want to be and are less likely to fudge on the results. For instance, if your goal is to use cognitive behavioral therapy to treat your insomnia, the goal "sleep better" is unspecific. If you are currently only getting an average of four hours of sleep, then you can call five hours of sleep "better". Yet, this amount of sleep is still not enough. Try to create goals of where you specifically want to be. In this instance, it is scientifically shown that humans need between seven and eight hours of sleep. Therefore, a specific goal would be "get seven hours of sleep every night and wake up at the same time every day."

Have Measurable Goals

It is important to know whether or not you are making progress toward your goals. This may be harder to track with some things such as depression than it is in business. But there are still certain ways you can measure your progress. If you are someone with depression who finds yourself no longer wanting to get out of bed, then every day you don't struggle with getting out of bed is a progress. You tell by the frequency of your depression symptoms improving how close you are getting toward your goal.

Keep Them Attainable

When creating business and life goals, some people will create goals that are so high that they are unattainable. For instance, the goal of becoming a millionaire within five years of graduating from college isn't likely to be attained. Thankfully, goals for the purpose of cognitive behavioral therapy are much more likely to be attained. You have power over your thoughts. You can become sober. You can get to a place where you are happy. You can overcome your fears. Your insomnia can be cured. All of these goals and more are attainable.

However, goals such as "never have another anxiety attack" and "never feel depressed again" are examples of unattainable goals. Remember, cognitive behavioral therapy will take time and work. You can't expect your mental health to be cured overnight.

Stay Realistic

Similar to keeping your goals attainable is to keep them realistic. You are capable of more than you know. While it may at times feel impossible to overcome your struggles, you can do it. Many people have overcome the same struggles in the past and with the tools provided by CBT, you are able to overcome them as well. However, you also need to stay realistic and you can do this by forgiving yourself.

If you punish yourself for having anxiety, depression, insomnia, or any number of other problems, then you are only straying further away from your goal. Stay positive, forgive yourself, and keep pushing forward.

Time Matters

Having a time frame for when you want to have your goal completed can help you track your progress and help you act. This is because if we simply say "someday I want to have a better life," then we are less likely to make progress in order to reach that "someday." Although, if we say "I want to have the confidence to answer the phone within a year," not only can we track our progress, but we can stay encouraged to put in the work needed to attain the goal.

Lastly, remember that people are more likely to reach their goals when they share it with someone who supports them. You don't want to share it with someone who is negative, overbearing, and unlikely to support you. This is more likely to discourage you. Instead, find a family member or friend who you know frequently support you and are likely to help encourage you and hold you accountable. If you don't have someone like this in your life, you can always find a group of people locally or online. For instance, an alcoholic may join Alcoholics Anonymous. You may even be able to find social media groups such as those on Facebook of other people going through similar struggles. If you can find someone in these groups that you connect with, you can both encourage one another.

After we know the goals we hope to achieve through cognitive behavioral therapy, it is time to begin to solve our problems. We can do this by consistently tinkering with our situations, moods, and thoughts. We are not going to improve our mental health simply by thinking of it as one big project that somehow needs to get done. Instead, we need to work on individual aspects of our health, relationships, and situations. By adjusting these smaller aspects, we are able to work on and improve the whole.

For instance, when a college or professional

football players are trying to improve their gameplay, the couch doesn't simply say "run further," "run faster," or "tackle better." Instead, the couch will give the players specific advice on how they can improve their gait when they run, how to improve their speed, and better ways to tackle successfully. By giving the players specific advice on specific problems, the couch is able to help the football players improve their overall ability.

Similarly, a professor wouldn't simply tell their students to study better or to improve their writing ability. Instead, a successful professor will walk their students through what exactly their students need to improve. They could show the students better resources to use and remind them that Wikipedia doesn't count as a source. If the student is struggling with spelling or grammar in their essays, the professor will point out exactly where the student is making mistake and give advice on what to do instead. By doing this, the professor is helping their students to improve exactly the way they need to, rather than giving ambiguous advice.

Similarly, you can use cognitive behavioral therapy to help you solve your individual problems and improve as a whole. You can achieve this by exploring your emotions and insecurities and then identifying the source of your problems and then finding solutions.

Cognitive behavioral therapy is known to be extremely beneficial and effective. However, the participants must be willing to put in effort and time to analyze their own thoughts and behaviors. This can be difficult, especially since people living with depression, anxiety, anger, or other emotional or mental issues are likely to dislike aspects of themselves. While nothing is wrong with them as a human being, these people may feel discouraged by looking at themselves honestly. But by working through this process, you can learn more about your internal state and how it can impact your outward behavior.

By learning to counteract your false and negative beliefs, you can replace them with positive and truthful beliefs. These can help improve a number of areas in life including all of your relationships, your work, sleep, and mental health.

For instance, people like Mary who are suffering from depression due to loss often develop a false belief that there is no point in communicating with others and that they can protect themselves by avoiding getting close to others. These people often also develop false ideas of their own worth, developing a negative self-esteem. As a result of these thoughts, these people often avoid social situations, begin to skip work or school when possible, and desire to do little else other than lying in bed.

We can use CBT in order to overcome these thoughts and behaviors. By using what is known as a functional analysis, we can gain a better understanding of our feelings, thoughts, and situations and how they impact our maladaptive behaviors. This isn't an easy process, especially for people who have a difficult time with introspection. But this process of developing a better sense of ourselves and gaining insight into our behavior is essential for improvement and treatment.

After developing a deeper understanding of ourselves, feelings, and thoughts, we are able to better focus on our behaviors. Due to our feelings and thoughts impacting our behaviors, we can create behavioral habits that only worsen our mental and emotional states. For instance, an addict will further believe that alcohol will make them feel better if they develop behavioral habits that support this false claim. Our feelings, thoughts, and behaviors can turn into a vicious cycle.

Thankfully, with cognitive behavioral therapy, we can learn practices that will help us overcome these behaviors and habits. We can learn to develop new habits, coping mechanisms, and plans to avoid falling back into our problematic behaviors. With CBT, we can make real change in our behaviors and prevent relapses. Whether you are trying to overcome depression or alcoholism, you can develop new behaviors that will help you better learn to cope and live a healthy and happy life.

You don't have to worry about making this change in behavior overnight. Your ingrained thoughts, emotions, and behaviors are not a light switch. You can't simply turn them off or on. But through a process of gradual steps to change these aspects, you can take steps toward your goal. Lydia could start by imagining herself in situations with dogs.

After she is able to do this well with plans on how to stay calm and in control of her emotions, she can move onto the next step. If some family or friends have friendly small dogs, she could try being around them while they are on a leash or in a kennel. Or she could even interact with puppies at an adoption event since puppies are much less frightening than a large full-grown dog.

As Lydia and other people utilizing CBT get more confident with each step, they can take the next one with more confidence. This gives the person security in seeing that they don't have to make a one-hundred and sixty-degree change overnight. They are also able to see their progress and learn that they can handle it.

In order to benefit from cognitive behavioral therapy, you need to work it into your daily life. After all, Mary, Lydia, and Matt will not improve if they only use the techniques they learn half of the time or even eighty percent of the time. It needs to be ingrained into your daily activities and mental state to make progress. Thankfully, there are some simple ways you can include CBT into your daily life and experience its many benefits.

Journal Throughout the Day

While by this point you already have a basic understanding of your thoughts and emotions, you need to stay on top of tracking them. A journal can help with this. Throughout the day, whenever you notice you are experiencing negative emotions or feelings track the following:

- Situation
- Mood
- Automatic Thoughts or Images
- Evidence that Supports my Thoughts
- Evidence that Disproves my Thoughts
- Alternative Healthy Thoughts
- New Mood

By journaling your situation, feelings, thoughts, and behaviors, you can gain a wider understanding of yourself. You may think that you already understand your triggers, feelings, and thoughts when you initially explored them as we described earlier. Yet, you will find that these can change over time and you may discover thoughts and behaviors you were previously ignorant of. By following through with journaling daily, you will be able to identify your emotions, insecurities, and the sources of your problems better so that you can take steps to further heal and improve.

Reconstruct your Cognition

Once we become aware of inaccurate or false ideas we hold on ourselves, behaviors, and the world, we can begin to learn why this false idea took root and why we began to believe it. This means that we can directly challenge these false ideas and replace them with the truth. For instance, a person who is in an accident and becomes disabled may develop the false idea that they are a shadow of their former selves and now are worth less than before. This can result in the person developing depression and anger at their situation.

But through cognitive behavioral therapy, they

can learn to directly challenge this false belief of themselves. They can learn that these negative inaccurate thoughts are a result of ableism in society and not because of themselves. After they accept this, they can begin to see that they aren't a shadow of their former selves and they are still the same person. The abilities of their body have no impact on their worth as a human being.

Think it Over to Overcome it

People living with anxiety, fear, and obsessive-compulsive disorder (OCD) can greatly benefit from this technique. With this method, a person follows through with a thought experiment, in which they imagine a situation that they are uncomfortable with. Imagine the worst case scenario that could happen. Allow the event to play through in your mind and then realize that even if the worst happened, it is likely to turn out okay. This method can also help people realize that the worst case scenario is unlikely and even if it did happen, they can make plans to handle it. Doing this takes the fear out of the situation and gives you the control over your fear.

Exposure Therapy

If you have a difficult time going to a specific place, interacting with people, or exposing yourself to other experiences, it is beneficial to expose yourself to it while you focus on staying calm. This means that if Lydia is interacting with dogs, she can remind herself of truthful thoughts and use coping mechanisms to stay calm. Mary can practice exposing herself to her loved ones without withdrawing due to her depression. Matt can learn to interact with people who often make him angry, while still controlling his temper. This type of therapy that goes along with CBT can especially be helpful for people who suffer from anxiety of obsessive-compulsive disorder.

It can be especially beneficial to journal during these situations, as it will help you refrain from the behavior you are trying to overcome. It can also help you to remind yourself of the truth rather than the lies that your brain is conditioned to believe.

It is important to expose ourselves to something that we fear or are uncomfortable with in order to overcome it.

Progressive Muscle Relaxation

This method, also known as PMR, should be familiar with people who practice meditation or mindfulness. With this technique, a person practices relaxing one group of muscles at a time until their entire body is relaxed. This can be completed on your own, with audio assistance, or even a smartphone app instructing you. Multiple studies have revealed the benefits of this practice. These studies have revealed that PMR has the ability to help decrease stress in mind and body more than other forms of relaxation. It has even been found to lower heart rate, reduce the cortisol hormone which increases stress, treats anxiety, and can even help improve the quality of life of cancer patients.

Breathe In and Out

Similarly to PMR, breathing techniques should be familiar to people who have used mindfulness or meditation. By utilizing regular, mathematics, and deep breathing exercises, a person can feel a sense of calm. This can allow them to find mental balance and more easily look at their situation and thoughts more clearly, accurately, and rationally.

The American Institute of Stress even explains that while many people will rest in front of the TV after a long and difficult day, this does little to relieve stress. The result is a buildup of stress over time, which impacts both our mental and physical health. In order to fight back against this daily stress, we need to utilize our body's natural ability to go into a state of relaxation.

This is known as the "relaxation response" and results in lowered blood pressure, decreased heart rate, relaxed muscle tension, improved oxygen delivery to the cells, an increase in the feel-good endorphins, detoxification of harmful chemicals and toxins, and of course decreased stress.

Our stress in life builds up, which can impact our mental health. This especially affects people with illnesses such as depression, obsessive-compulsive disorder, anxiety, panic disorder, alcoholism, insomnia, and much more! We need to deal with this stress both mentally and physically in order to lessen these problems. By utilizing deep breathing, your body can go into the relaxation response, physically allowing your body to remove stress and relax. But this process also helps to clear your mind and can help you further along in cognitive behavioral therapy.

When we are in a stressed or disturbed state of mind, our situation seems worse than it actually is. This will affect our emotions, thoughts, and behavior. But by utilizing deep breathing and the other techniques mentioned here, you can find a state of calm in both mind and body. This will allow you to correct the false ideas in your mind, find the truth, and calmly figure out solutions to any problems you may be experiencing.

It is important to remember that it is not the events that happen to us that control us, rather the meaning we allow them to hold over us. If we allow these events to control our emotions, thoughts, and behaviors, we can begin to believe the false negative thoughts as truth.

Just like Mary believes that there is no point in interacting with other people because they may die. Or how Mary believes that she is worth less than other people. While these thoughts may have been small when they first began, as time went on, these thoughts grew and took control. This turns her feelings, thoughts, and behaviors into a vicious cycle that reinforce one another.

But if Mary learns to take control of these feelings, thoughts, and behaviors through cognitive behavioral therapy, then they will lose their power over her. She may still struggle with these thoughts at first or from time to time, but gradually she will come to see them as false. The more consistently Mary journals, interact with other people, practices muscle relaxation and deep breathing, and visualizes day is going well, then the more confidence she will have in herself and the truth. She will learn to believe that she does have worth and that while no living thing can continue to live forever, there is still meaning in connections and interacting with others. She can begin to enjoy and love life again the more she fights back against the dysfunctional thought processes brought on by depression.

Through this process, we can overcome our automatic thoughts that tell us lies such as *"I completely failed," "I can't do this,"* and *"Nobody likes me.*

But even if you aren't someone who is living with a major depressive disorder, anxiety, disorder, or a number of other disorders, you can still benefit from cognitive behavioral therapy. In fact, this type of therapy can help anyone in their daily lives. Whether you struggle with self-acceptance, low self-esteem, or anger management on a daily basis or only occasionally, CBT can help you develop better thought processes, coping mechanisms, and behaviors.

Improve Your Self-Esteem

How we think about ourselves affects every area of our lives. Our confidence, feelings, thoughts, and behaviors can all be impacted by what we think of ourselves. A person with a healthy self-esteem can accurately judge their abilities, how those around them feel, and can regulate their emotions and thoughts accordingly. On the other hand, someone with low self-esteem is likely to be highly critical of themselves, incorrectly believe that the people around them must dislike them, and they are less likely to act on positive opportunities. However, cognitive behavioral therapy has been studied extensively for self-esteem and it has been found to be the most effective type of treatment.

For treating self-esteem, CBT can help us recognize the negative and false thinking habits we fall into and replace them with positive truthful thoughts. By replacing our distorted ideas of ourselves with truthful ideas, we can learn to see that we have value, that we aren't a failure, and that there are people out there who genuinely like and care for us.

When a person has low self-esteem, they are likely to avoid activities that they feel they may fail at. This means that they could avoid social interactions, higher education, a challenging job, or even a simple hobby. This results in the person having fewer rewarding experiences and can lead to depression. By learning to alter behavior and re-engage in these activities, you can break the cycle and learn to fully enjoy activities. You don't have to be perfect for an experience to be worthwhile, valuable, and enjoyable.

People with self-esteem issues often have little assertiveness. Training to increase assertiveness can be combined with cognitive behavioral therapy. This will help a person make their feelings and requests known better, and in the process, they can begin to feel their own importance rather than worthlessness.

These same people often struggle with feeling helpless and powerless in situations. But with thinking over situations before they happen and utilizing problem-solving technique, they can learn how to overcome their struggles. This can give the person a boost of encouragement and a further sense of self-agency. By creating a plan ahead, you will not have to be stressed at the moment when something occurs.

If someone struggles with social skills due to their low self-esteem, they can learn to practice. Rather than avoiding situations, throw yourself into them with people that you feel comfortable with. As you learn more social skills, you can begin to interact with a wider range of people. This will continue to boost your confidence while increasing your ability to interact with others.

Increase Your Self-Acceptance

While a lack of self-acceptance and self-esteem often go hand in hand and can be treated similarly, there are slight differences. Self-esteem is often a person having a disbelief in their abilities, whereas, self-acceptance is often a person struggling to accept their thoughts and mental state.

Cognitive behavioral therapy can be used to help patients to stop denying, avoiding, and struggling with their emotions. Instead, they can learn to accept their feelings and find appropriate ways in which to react to them. When a person begins to accept what they feel, deal with the emotions, they can then move forward in life. This is especially helpful for people who live with mental illness or who are overcoming trauma.

By working with a psychologist, they can listen to you and help you learn how to process your emotions in a healthy manner, accept them, and move on. This can help you to improve your relationships, find joy in being yourself, and overcome traumatic life events. You can also practice this to an extent on your own by using the emotional thought journal method we have taught you. This method can help you learn which emotions and thoughts are true and which are not. This is extremely important because by suppressing our emotions, we gradually develop more stress and harmful beliefs.

Once you make a commitment to accept yourself, then you can face any issues you are facing, become more confident, increase your optimism, overcome your past, and create new behaviors that are based on truth, acceptance, and your personal goals.

Manage Your Anger

Everyone experiences anger to some degree. However, some people experience it more frequently or in outbursts. This is one of the problems that Matt deals with. While Matt is generally well-liked and enjoys a vibrant social life, sometimes he feels as if he can't control his anger. When he feels disrespected or criticized, then that turns all around him red and he practically explodes. When Matt gets angry, everyone around him knows it, whether he is at home or in a restaurant.

But with cognitive behavioral therapy, you can target your anger and the thoughts and behaviors that are tied to it. As you progress with using CBT, you can find that your anger gradually decreases, your periods of anger last for a shorter period of time, you feel it more mildly, and you will gain control over your emotions, thoughts, and behaviors.

If you are struggling to overcome your anger, then you can rate its strength, frequency, and duration in your CBT journal. From a zero to one-hundred, meaningless to more, rate how strongly you feel your anger, how frequently, and how long it lasts. During the beginning, you may need to track this daily. But the later you get in your journey and learn to overcome your anger, you can begin to track it less frequently.

Everyone can get angry over different events. While one person may get angry about being interrupted, another may patiently wait to continue what they had been saying. This is often because our anger can be based on our past. If we have a history of being treated poorly or abused, then those situations in the future are more likely to cause us to become defensive.

This is because anger often goes along with the subconscious belief that we can protect ourselves from harm, abuse, or mistreatment if we confront the person, action, or circumstance that is upsetting us.

To help you better understand your anger and the reasons behind it, remember a recent circumstance when you were angry and journal it. If you are unable to accurately recall what happened, journal your anger the next time it occurs. First, journal the strength, frequency, and duration, then journal the situation, mood, automatic thoughts or images, evidence that supports your thoughts, evidence that disproves your thoughts, alternative healthy thoughts, and your new mood after the evaluation.

By logging this, you can learn what was going through your mind when you were angry and develop a new understanding of yourself. This will allow you to better manage or express your anger and learn more constructive ways to manage it.

Chapter 4: Cognitive Behavioral Therapy in Action

By this point, you know well how to utilize cognitive behavioral therapy in general circumstances. But you may want more detail on how to find the most benefit if you are living with a specific condition. This is because CBT is not a single method. Rather, it is a combination of many techniques that can be altered depending on the condition that is being treated. In this chapter, we will go over how you can use CBT to help with panic disorder, insomnia, bipolar disorder, obsessive-compulsive disorder, self-harm, post-traumatic stress disorder, and more. Combining the tips in this chapter with the basic elements of CBT will help you get the most out of your treatment and find relief.

Insomnia

Sleep medication is a common treatment for short-term bouts of insomnia. This can be especially helpful for people who are going through a period of grief or high stress. But the options for people with long-term chronic insomnia are limited. There may be some newer medications, but these are ineffective on many people. They can also cause it so that people become unable to sleep without relying on the prescription.

But cognitive behavioral therapy is an approved treatment for the treatment of insomnia and has been shown to be highly effective. If you are worried about side effects of medication, becoming dependent, or unable to find a medication that works for you, then CBT may be the answer you are looking for.

Unlike prescriptions, CBT can help to address the cause of insomnia, rather than masking the symptoms. Although people with especially difficult cases of insomnia may benefit from a combination of both prescriptions and CBT.

It is important to remember that cognitive behavioral therapy isn't an overnight fix. This is a process and does take both time and effort.

Professional cognitive behavioral therapy involves regular visits with a trained psychologist who can customize your treatment plan. They will do this by assessing your sleep habits through a journal that you keep.

A U.S. Navy swim and safety instructor, Caroline developed a terrible case of insomnia while recovering from a knee surgery. The pain of her knee was excruciating, which led to her requiring medication that made her sleepy. Between the sleepiness from the pain medication and doctors' orders to stay in bed, Caroline found it difficult to stay awake throughout the day without drifting off to sleep. Yet, these naps greatly impacted her sleep schedule.

Before long, Caroline found that it was nearly impossible to fall asleep and stay asleep at nighttime. Even after her knee was healed and she was able to go back to working with the Navy, Caroline could not stop napping during the day. Every day as soon as she got home from work, she would fall asleep. This led to her being unable to sleep soundly throughout the night and continued to leave her exhausted in a brutal cycle.

After trying a variety of prescription sleep aids, Caroline found that none of them helped her except for Ambien. Finally, she was no longer feeling fatigued and sleepy at work and she was able to sleep through the night! Despite this, Caroline knew that she couldn't stay on the medication for the remainder of her life. This was soon proven when her insurance would no longer cover the Ambien. This is because it is a medication specifically for short-term use, therefore, the insurance provider would not approve it for a long-term case of insomnia.

Caroline was soon recommended to the Clinical Assistant Professor in the Department of Psychiatry at Brown Medical School, who was also a Director of Behavioral Sleep Medicine in Rhode Island. While she was hesitant to see a psychiatrist, Caroline knew she had to do something so she set up an appointment with Dr. Donn Posner.

Caroline still learned that cognitive behavioral therapy wasn't an overnight easy cure. Instead, she found that the first six weeks of treatment, she was getting very little sleep. But after she kept a sleeping journal, Dr. Posner was able to review it and help Caroline find how to cure her insomnia.

It wasn't easy, but Caroline learned that she had to completely stop taking naps and couldn't go to bed early any longer. In fact, she wasn't allowed to go to bed until midnight. Without her early evening bedtime and naps, Caroline was finding it incredibly difficult to stay awake until her bedtime. It was the hardest six weeks of her life. Thankfully, Caroline soon started to sleep better and as she did, she was allowed to back up her bedtime so that she wasn't going to sleep as late.

By looking over Caroline's sleep journal over the following weeks, Dr. Posner was able to further customize her sleep routine to help lessen her insomnia. He found that using stimulus control was important. With this portion of CBT for insomnia, he found that she needed to spend less time in her bedroom when she wasn't sleeping. This even means that if Caroline found she was unable to fall asleep, that she was supposed to leave her bedroom and not come back until she felt that she was ready to sleep.

She was also supposed to practice better sleep hygiene. This entailed Caroline having to avoid stimulants such as caffeine, alcohol, and tobacco before bedtime, as well as avoiding exercise close to bedtime and sleeping in a cool and completely dark room.

Professionals can find many problems that an individual may not recognize their sleep routine. For instance, Caroline was a frequent offender of clock watching. Many people who suffer from insomnia will begin to stare at the clock at night, watching the hours tick by. But this is dangerous because it becomes a part of your routine. Even worse, it leads to frustration and worry which are only known to worsen insomnia.

Caroline was instructed by Dr. Posner to completely stop looking at her clock after going to bed. Therefore, she covered her clocks in her room so that she could still be woken by the alarm, but couldn't see the time.

Another task that Caroline was given by Dr. Posner was to stop working close to bedtime. This only wakes up the brain, when it should be settling down for bedtime. She was also told to avoid watching TV in the evening as that has a similar effect. Caroline stopped bringing her work home with her in the evening. Instead, she would spend her time relaxing with a book or painting.

After six weeks of working through insomnia-specific cognitive behavioral therapy, Caroline found that her sleep had greatly improved and was only continuing to get better. While she originally needed to see Dr. Posner on a weekly basis, she now only rarely has checkup appointments although she is staying on top of relapse prevention care. With this, Caroline can ensure that she sticks to the cognitive behavioral therapy tactics she was taught and prevent another bout of insomnia.

Caroline does this by not compensating for the loss of sleep, beginning her sleep restriction phase if she finds she has insomnia for more than a few days, and avoiding stimulating substances and activities before bed.

Cognitive behavioral therapy can also help you to eliminate negative worries and thoughts that might keep you lying awake all night. This is one of the most common causes of insomnia. Because of this, CBT targets the direct reason that you are unable to sleep. Following is a list and description of the most common CBT treatment options for insomnia.

Relaxation Training

The use of meditation, muscle relaxation, visualization, and other relaxation techniques to calm or overcome negative thinking. This can be practiced throughout the day as well to help relieve anxiety, which will naturally lessen it at night as well.

Stimulus Therapy

There are many factors in our lives that can make our mind avoid sleep. This can include the time we spend in our room, the naps we take, and what time we get up in the morning. As an example, it is often recommended to limit bedroom activity to sex and sleep. Similarly, only go to bed when you are tired and if you are unable to fall asleep within twenty minutes, then go to another room until you feel you are able to sleep. Try to get out of bed at the same time every day and try to greatly limit naps.

Sleep Hygiene

This process involves limiting lifestyle factors that interfere with sleep. You will want to either avoid stimulants within a few hours of bedtime or avoid them completely. Some people may be unable to sleep without a bedtime snack and that's okay. Try to engage in relaxing activities such as reading, writing, listening to calming music, painting, or taking a bath before bed.

It is imperative to avoid working, watching TV, doing the computer, exercising, and other stimulating activities before bed.

Paradoxical Inattention

Also known as remaining passively awake, this process involves a person resting while avoiding trying to sleep. This is because when we are actively trying to sleep, we can become anxious and worry, which only worsens insomnia. Instead, it is important to be able to lie in bed without actively trying to sleep. Don't worry, the sleep will come on its own, you can't make it happen.

Biofeedback

Often used alongside relaxation training, biofeedback is more complex than the other methods.

However, it can be highly successful. With this method, a person is given a device that can detect brainwave frequency, muscle tension, and other biological aspects. With biofeedback, you are taught how to adjust your own brain waves, blood pressure, muscle tension, heart rate, and body temperature.

It may take some practice and concentration, but some people find that within only a few sessions they are able to get the hang of it. Using this method, you can directly impact various body functions in order to help your body be in a state where it can more easily fall asleep.

There are many components involved in cognitive behavioral therapy for insomnia. Although many people don't use all of these components, you may combine several of them to take control of your sleep and health.

Anxiety

Throughout this book, we have frequently discussed how we need to replace our false thoughts with thoughts of truth. This is especially important with people living with one of a number of anxiety disorders. Often, people with these disorders need to learn to let go of guilt, embarrassment, and anger over their pasts. How to be more realistic and not hold themselves to perfection, how to overcome misconceptions they may have about their self-worth and abilities, how to deal with procrastination, and how to become more assertive when needed.

This is especially needed with anxiety disorders because people with anxiety have developed automatic thoughts that are negative and inaccurate from reality. These thoughts only increase anxiety and lessen their ability to cope with life.

If you are someone living with an anxiety disorder, you have most likely heard someone simply tell you to "think more positively." Sadly, you know that it isn't that easy. If it were, you would have resolved your problems long ago. Instead, your brain is in a constant state of anxiety and negativity that is difficult to overcome. Just telling yourself to be less anxious and trying to think of something else doesn't resolve the problem of your brain.

But with practice and commitment, you can use cognitive behavioral therapy to retrain your brain. While at first, this may simply mean that when you notice a negative thought, you analyze it and turn it into a realistic positive or neutral thought, over time it can become more powerful and easier.

As the process becomes easier, you can continue to challenge more difficult thoughts until this feels like second nature. Gradually, your neural pathways and memory processes will physically alter. This will naturally lead you to feel different. You will find that it is easier to be optimistic, you will find yourself anxious less often, and anxiety will be easier to overcome. It takes patience and consistency, but it is well worth it.

Systematic desensitization is one of the most common types of treatment used in cognitive behavioral therapy for anxiety disorders. This type of CBT treatment involves a person gradually exposing themselves to situations which often cause anxiety. Over time, the person will learn to cope. These situations will begin to affect the person less and they can even move onto more difficult anxiety challenges. This process is scary at first, but it isn't as simple as facing your fears and toughening up. Instead, you work on very gradually working through a step-by-step process.

For instance, if someone is afraid of heights, they wouldn't immediately begin by bungee jumping off of a cliff to face their fears. This would only worsen their fear and make it more difficult to overcome. Instead, a trained therapy, psychologist or psychiatrist can help you work through these fears at a pace that is right for you.

This type of therapy often begins with visualization. A person with a phobia of heights can begin by imagining themselves in a situation that would usually frighten them. As imagining these situations becomes easier, they can very slowly begin to transition the therapy to real-world applications.

Although this must be done very slowly to prevent the process from backfiring. This means a person with a fear of heights would most likely try standing on a short footstool or going onto the second story of a building.

If someone is unable to make appointments to a psychologist either due to logistics or their own anxiety, there are still options to work with a trained professional. In recent years, CBT over the internet has become increasingly popular. Research has even found that it can be highly successful and is more suited to online use than other forms of therapy.

If you have an anxiety disorder and hope to use cognitive behavioral therapy for treatment, there are a few key factors to attain success. Studies show how successful CBT can largely rely on the individual and their willingness to confront uncomfortable or difficult thoughts and complete homework projects. It may be daunting, but CBT has been shown to be highly effective in people with anxiety if they are willing to work for it. Thankfully, the results have been shown to be well worth the work that they require and are long-lasting.

Panic Disorder

Some people may assume that anxiety disorders and panic disorder are the same things. But while they can both become debilitating, they are different. The best way to describe this is that anxiety is the type of fear that you experience when you are worried that you are going to fail a class in college and will have to repeat a year. Whereas panic attacks are the type of fear you would experience if someone is breaking into your house and you are in imminent danger.

Yet, panic disorders happen when there is no present danger. They can be triggered by something as small as someone touching your arm. Everyone's panic attack triggers vary. They are usually accompanied by a variety of physical symptoms. These can include dizziness, shortness of breath, a racing heart rate, feeling faint, trembling, nausea, chills or hot flashes, chest pain, choking sensations, or sweating. They can also make people feel as if they are dying, a feeling of detachment, or as if they are going crazy.

These attacks are sudden and usually last

between one and ten minutes. The person experiences a strong urge to run away and reach safety due to our natural flight or fight response. At first, these attacks often are triggered by no known cause, but over time, they can become isolated to certain situations. For instance, a person may develop panic attacks due to flying, elevators, leaving home, or a number of other situations. If left untreated, they can often result in anxiety or a reliance on drugs or alcohol to ease the symptoms. Many people become disabled due to panic attacks and are no longer able to manage to work.

There has been significant research proving the effectiveness of CBT on panic disorder. In fact, after twelve weeks of thirteen small group sessions participants improved greatly. Comprehensive assessments were conducted on all participants both prior to therapy, midway, and once it was completed. By the end of the twelve weeks, every one of the participants was free of their spontaneous panic attacks and was able to qualify as high functioning. This type of therapy has been shown to greatly outperform other treatment methods including medication.

The CBT treatment plans for panic disorder often involve mindfulness, exposure therapy, relaxation training, cognitive restructuring to replace anxiety-provoking thoughts with more balanced thoughts, and stress reduction to help a person learn to react to situations more calmly.

Depression and Suicidal Ideation

Life has many ups and downs that can lead people to develop a case of depression. As many as fourteen million adults in America suffer from a major depressive disorder at some point in their lives. While for some people this is only a temporary problem, other's struggle with depression for their entire lives. This can make people feel lonely, hopeless, and empty. But there is no need to suffer silently. There is always someone who can help you, whether it is a family member, friend, someone online, or a psychologist.

While depression can become disabling and even lead to suicidal ideation (which means thoughts of suicide) or attempted suicide, CBT has been shown to be an effective treatment. Whether you are suffering from moderate or severe depression, cognitive behavioral therapy has been shown time and again to be successful in treatment. This therapy can either be done as the sole method of treatment or combined with anti-depressants.

When treating depression, your therapist will focus on helping you to overcome your negative thought processes and changing them to something more balanced. This takes time, but over time it can change your brain's shape and synapses, not only mentally helping your brain improve, but physically aiding it as well.

Addictions and Obsessions

Whether you are suffering from drug or alcohol addiction, cognitive behavioral therapy can help. It may seem overwhelming, but with the process of CBT, an overwhelming problem can be turned into small manageable pieces. A therapist or psychologist will have the ability to analyze you personally along with your situation, difficulties, and other problems. Your therapy plan can be customized so that it is approachable and while still helpful both in the short-term and long-term. Just like with other forms of CBT, people using it for alcohol or drug addiction will be asked to practice homework. This homework is most often the process of analyzing your own thoughts and feelings and turning false negative thoughts into balanced thoughts.

There are three main factors that are frequently focused on this form of CBT. These are recognizing, avoiding, and coping.

Your psychologist will help you learn to recognize the instances that you are most likely to indulge your addiction.

You will then learn to avoid these situations when it is appropriate or feasible.

Lastly, you will learn to cope with a wide range of behaviors caused by addiction. You can be taught how to find better self-control, explore the positive and negative effects of your addiction, monitor yourself to recognize cravings and weaknesses early on, and how to develop strategies for when you are most likely to engage in your addiction.

Addiction can be overwhelming and feel as if it is impossible to overcome. Although, research clearly shows the benefits of cognitive behavioral therapy in the treatment of both alcohol and drug addiction. In fact, the skills and benefits people learn from CBT have been shown to remain long after the participants finish their therapy.

Obsessive-Compulsive Disorder

Obsessive-compulsive disorder, otherwise known as OCD, is often thought to simply be people who are prone to cleaning or organizing. However, someone simply being picky when it comes to organization or cleaning is completely different from the level of obsessiveness that OCD causes.

Firstly, OCD does not mean someone tends to clean or organize. Some people may, but there are many other ways in which OCD may manifest. OCD is characterized by persistent and repeated unwanted thoughts. Even if a person tries to ignore them, they often are unable to. This can lead to rituals or behaviors that are compulsive. These compulsions may be so overwhelming that a person who feels the need to wash their hands may end up washing them until they are raw and bleeding on a daily basis.

Some of the common obsessions with OCD include thoughts of harm coming to you, worry that you may harm someone else, aggressive impulses, unwanted sexual thoughts, fear of contamination, and needing things orderly or symmetrical.

Thankfully, cognitive behavioral therapy has been shown to be one of the most effective forms of treatment of OCD. The research has shown that a significant seventy-five percent of patients with OCD improve greatly from CBT and some studies even have the number as high as eighty percent. Due to the success of CBT with few side effects or negative aspects, it has been chosen as the top choice for managing OCD by the Center for Anxiety Disorders and Trauma, the National Institute for Health and Clinical Excellence, and other originations.

When first beginning therapy, a person will be

asked to list and describe their various compulsions and obsessions. They will rank them so that the therapist can easily see what is most difficult for each individual. Next, they will be asked to give recent examples of when their OCD was more severe. It is important to go into detail of the thoughts, images, urges, and doubts that may have occurred during that time.

The goal of cognitive behavioral therapy isn't to get rid of the thoughts that occur alongside OCD. Instead, a therapist can help you learn to cope with them. They can help overturn these urges and thoughts so that they no longer control them or frighten them. The thoughts that once used to control their life will turn into ideal passing. They will no longer have to act on them in order to feel relief.

A good therapist or psychologist is able to learn how an individual's OCD works, what keeps it going, the ideas behind it, and how to change it into something manageable. The treatment of OCD may not be easy, no matter what type of therapy a person chooses. But, with cognitive behavioral therapy and a well-trained professional, it is possible to find relief.

Eating Disorders and Negative Body Image

Whether you live with anorexia, bulimia, binge eating, or another eating disorder, cognitive behavioral therapy may help. In fact, out of all the uses for CBT, eating disorders have been shown to be one of the most effective cases for this type of treatment and therapy. Largely because CBT focuses both on the mental and physical aspects of eating disorders. CBT does not only help treat one type of eating disorder, as it has been found to help all types.

In therapy, people will be taught both how their cognition affects their body image, self-evaluation, self-worth, perfectionism, and core beliefs. They will also be taught how to manage the behavioral factors of eating disorders such as purging, binge-eating, self-harm, weighing, and other actions.

A therapist or psychologist can help educate you to help you learn the skills and education you need in order to gain a more balanced understanding of yourself. There are three main phases — the behavioral, the cognitive, and the maintenance.

During the behavioral phase, the therapist can help you to balance your eating and eliminate your individual symptoms based on your specific eating disorder. Although a person's emotions often worsen during this portion of the therapy, a therapist can help. By teaching you coping mechanisms, strategies, and important tools to manage your feelings both in sessions and at home, your psychologist can help you move onto the next phase of treatment.

During the cognitive phase, the psychologist will focus on changing your thought patterns. By identifying and targeting harmful and negative thoughts such as "I can only be happy if I lose weight," you can gain a new understanding and lessen your desires to continue in the harmful behavior. Your negative thoughts can be replaced with balanced alternatives such as "my worth is not dependent on my size or the number on the scale."

Once you begin the maintenance phase, your psychologist will focus on helping you reduce known triggers, the prevention of relapses, and teach you tools to maintain your hard-earned progress.

Post-Traumatic Stress Disorder

"One of the key factors that allow CBT to be one of the most effective theories when working with clients with PTSD is its ability to focus on

processing thoughts, beliefs, and emotions about individual activating events. The ABC model allows the client to isolate the traumatic event and begin to dispute maladaptive thoughts, emotions, and behaviors associated with that event without being overwhelmed with other life events." - Felicia Jessup, M.A, NCC, LPC

Everyone will experience stressful and upsetting events during their lifetime. But when these events are especially upsetting or stressful, they may turn into a traumatic experience which is incredibly distressing. The loss of a loved one, an intense surgery, an armed robbery, all of these events and more can be traumatic.

When situations are especially horrific, dangerous, or lead to a sense of helplessness, then a person may develop a long-term psychological scar. This can be caused by a wide variety of situations, but some of the most common include abuse, sexual assault, war experience, victimization from a crime, serious injury, and natural disasters.

While it cannot be predicted who will develop PTSD, those who suffer worse trauma are more likely to develop this condition. Nobody is immune to mental health conditions, PTSD, or otherwise.

There are multiple theories on PTSD and

understanding these theories can help during the treatment process. The emotional processing theory by Rauch and Foa from 2006 suggests that people who have experienced trauma may develop unhealthy associations due to the experience. This can cause the person to develop further stress when they encounter something that reminds them of the experience. These same people may also develop maladaptive cognition and distorted views.

Thankfully, with the use of the cognitive model that we have previously discussed, also known as the ABC model, along with exposure therapy conducted by a trained professional, many people are able to find relief.

A therapist may use a variety of elements found within cognitive behavioral therapy to help their patients with PTSD. Although, just as the quote by Ms. Felicia Jessup mentions, one of the most successful components of CBT is its ability to focus on a person's thoughts, beliefs, and emotions about the traumatic event. Ms. Jessup utilized this method frequently while working as a civilian military liaison for the U.S Air Force. She would use the cognitive model or ABC model to help her patients identify and re-evaluate their unhealthy thinking patterns or distortions. These thoughts such as expecting catastrophic events, negative thinking that overrides positive thinking, and self-blame for the traumatic event can be re-conceptualized. This allows the patient to gain a better understanding, not only of the traumatic event but also of themselves and their ability to cope.

Within cognitive behavioral therapy, a therapist can slowly help a patient work through exposure therapy. This is done in a safe environment and with the patient's full consent, so as to not cause further trauma. By exposing the patient to reminders of their trauma, whether through visualization, sounds, or other methods in a controlled environment, they are able to heal. This process can give the patient increased self-confidence and they can learn to reduce the need to avoid or escape similar reminders.

By helping a patient learn about how trauma may affect them, relaxation techniques for managing stress, and planning solutions for uncomfortable or triggering situations, a therapist can further improve a patient's control, confidence, and healing.

Chapter 5: Dialectical Behavioral Therapy in Action

If you previously heard of CBT prior to picking up this book, then you might have heard of DBT or dialectical behavioral therapy as well. But what does the term 'dialectical' even mean? This term is defined as two opinions or forces that may appear to be opposites working together synergistically.

This means that while both acceptance and change may seem to be opposites, in DBT a patient is taught both to accept themselves where they are at and to change so that they may attain their goals. This method was developed by Marsha Linehan Ph.D., ABPP, and uses elements of emotional regulation, mindfulness, interpersonal effectiveness, and distress tolerance. The goal of this therapy is to help patients create goals, build a life that they feel is worthwhile in living, and decrease harmful behaviors.

While this treatment was originally created for people who are suicidal and diagnosed with borderline personality disorder (BPD), it has been found to be beneficial for many other individuals as well. The four elements of DBT in detail include:

- Emotional Regulation: The ability to reduce painful emotions and vulnerability while changing the emotions that you desire.

- Mindfulness: The practice of learning to be fully present and aware during the moment.

- Interpersonal Effectiveness: Begin to ask other for what you need and also learn the ability to say 'no' when needed while still retaining solid relationships with others.

- Distress Tolerance: Learn that you don't have to change painful situations, rather learn how to tolerate them.

These elements of DBT are usually taught in four different methods which include skills training group, personalized treatment, phone coaching, and team consultation.

The skills training group in DBT is centered on helping the patients learn behavioral skills. These training groups meet once weekly for a twenty-four week period and may even sometimes be repeated for a full year of training. During this time, groups function similarly to a class and the participants are given homework to help them integrate their newly learned skills during daily life.

While the participants are already done a once-weekly group training session, they will also attend a once-weekly therapy session. The purpose of this is to increase the patient's motivation, set specific goals, and help them further apply the skills they learned in the group.

Between sessions of individual therapy, the patients are able to contact their therapist on the phone for immediate help. This is especially influential in people who live with incredibly difficult diagnoses that are obstructing their daily lives.

The team consultation portion is meant to help the therapists and to support them with patients who may have increasingly complex and difficult to treat conditions. This team of people helps the therapist to stay motivated and may give advice when needed. The team consultation group typically will meet once weekly.

The therapist will organize the patient's care into four stages and these stages are based on the individual person's timeline and behavior. Rather than having a set period of time for each stage, this gives the therapist the ability to spend as much or little time within a stage as the patient requires.

The first stage is when a patient first begins DBT and because of this, they often describe their mental state as "hell". They may even try to self-harm, attempt suicide, or use alcohol or drugs. This stage ends when the patient is no longer self-destructive and begins to show control of their behavior.

During the second stage, the patient may no longer be an immediate danger to themselves. Although, they continue to suffer and feel as if they are living in quiet desperation. The second stage ends once the patient is able to move on from quiet desperation and begins to experience emotions fully.

The third stage comprises of the patients learning to create goals, find peace, build a sense of self-respect, and experience joy. The goal for this stage is that the patient is able to happily live a life of both happiness and unhappiness.

Stage four is for people who are looking for a deeper spiritual meaning in their lives. This stage creates a deeper sense of fulfillment for people who are unable to settle into a life of regular ups and downs that come and go throughout life. The goal of this stage is to help patients move on from feeling incomplete to experiencing a fulfilled sense of joy and freedom.

Why are we talking about DBT in an book focusing on CBT? Well, because dialectical behavioral therapy was created based off of CBT. When Dr. Linehan and other therapists first created this form of therapy, they included many CBT techniques. This includes homework, behavioral analysis, skills training, and a behavioral rating scale. They created this because some patients who struggle with the need to change and becoming overwhelmed didn't feel as if their needs were being met. But after Dr. Linehan and the other therapists looked over video recordings of their sessions, they noticed similarities in what helped these struggling patients. These patients required a plan that helped them learn to manage their pain and find purpose in living. After beginning the new therapy method, these patients continued on with therapy, improved more quickly, and their relationship with their therapists improved.

Therefore, DBT has many of the same benefits of cognitive behavioral therapy. Although, if a person finds that CBT isn't enough for their mental health needs, then they may need to try dialectical behavioral therapy.

A psychologist who trained under Dr. Linehan learns how to effectively use DBT. Dr. Kelly Koerner encourages people to use aspects of cognitive and dialectical behavioral therapies in their daily lives. One instance they recommend using these therapies in is when we are stuck between two opinions or courses of action. This could mean that if you are struggling with a circumstance, but you are unable to change it, the techniques of DBT can help. You can find a way to either accept or change the circumstance.

During a lecture for the National Education Alliance for Borderline Personality Disorder, Dr. Koerner discussed how these techniques can be integrated into daily life. As she discussed how DBT can help people, she led the listeners through the process of using it.

- Identify the two competing positions. This will vary from person to person, but for instance, say the positions are to either adopt a dog or adopt a cat.

- Fully examine both positions in an honest and straightforward manner. You want to make a list of what the pros or the truths of both sides.

- Focus on your body, find your center of gravity, and focus on deep slow breathing. Do this until you have developed a calm and grounded feeling of balance.

- Honestly ask yourself what your purpose in life is and how the person who you want to be would rectify or decide on the situation. What matters most to you? Years down the road when you are older, how will you feel about your choice? Focus on keeping grounded in these thoughts.

- While staying grounded, allow yourself to examine your feelings and all of the truths regarding your dilemma. We have all been shaped by our environment and how we were raised and this affects our opinions. Consider the person from the opposing opinion, how they formed their opinion, and what may be shaping it.

- In order to see what all led to the conflict, create a chain analysis. This can show all the ongoing emotions such as anger, jealousy, or disappointment. Although, it can also show other emotions that led up to the forming of opinions such as compassion, empathy, generosity, and kindness.

- Finally, you can end by verbally validating both positions while fleshing out possible solutions for each side. When dealing with conflict, you should try to combine the solutions so that it is a compromise for both people.

Dr. Koerner stresses that even if we are unable to see a solution immediately, we can still learn to accept the circumstance. We can focus on demonstrating compassion.

Anxiety

Our emotions are vital in the way our lives function. Yet, while emotions such as fear can be helpful when we are in a time of danger, sometimes we may develop anxiety disorders where these emotions are caused by unknown triggers. This anxiety, rather than helping us to survive in a dangerous situation, simply makes life into a miserable challenge. Even if we try to simply "think happy thoughts," the anxiety won't go away.

Thankfully, with dialectical behavioral therapy, we can learn cognitive and emotional skills which we can then apply to our lives. Even if our emotions are incredibly difficult and distressing, DBT is equipped to handle them. By working your way through DBT, you can learn to regulate your emotions and how you choose to express them.

Rather than fighting the reality of a situation, you can practice a deep mindfulness and techniques to better tolerate your distress. These will enable you to be able to accept situations and events better. There are many ways you can practice this. Some people count to ten, others use breathing exercises, while others still will hold an ice cube to help them focus at the moment, guiding them toward acceptance.

By using the skills taught for emotional regulation, you will be able to calmly observe and describe your emotions. This can be accomplished by solving the problem to thereby change the circumstances and your emotions, acting opposite of the way you desire or by double checking the facts of a given situation.

But before you try to influence or change your emotions using DBT, it is imperative that you first understand why these emotions are rising and where they are coming from. This is one of the main points of DBT and is one of the distinguishing factors between it and CBT. By non-judgmentally and mindfully analyzing a situation or describing your emotions, you can more effectively differentiate between fact and fiction. This will allow you to more calmly manage and control your emotions. This process is one of the reasons why DBT has been shown to be so successful in patients with anxiety and other disorders.

Depression and Suicidal Ideation

During 2002, a study was published in the American Journal of Geriatric Psychiatry. In this study, it was found that DBT is an effective therapy and treatment for depression. The results were that an astonishing seventy-one percent of the participants were free of all symptoms caused by depression by the completion of the study.

While DBT may not have been specifically created for the treatment of depression, rather it was for borderline personality disorder, it can be a significant help for those suffering from this condition. This is because the core principles and skills taught by DBT are tolerance and validation, both of which are something that people living with depression could use more of. These people often feel an overwhelming sense of loss, worthlessness, hopelessness, and sadness. Every aspect of their lives is affected and all too often they don't even want to get out of bed because that means another day living with depression will start again.

Whether or not people with depression are living in a toxic environment in which they are verbally abused or they are constantly berating themselves, circumstances in a person's life will affect their depression. However, with DBT, they can learn coping mechanisms to enable them to directly address the problems in their lives.

Journaling or the use of diary cards is another major component of DBT which can be an invaluable option for people with depression. These can help a person to better track what coping mechanisms they are using, behaviors that affect them, and their invalidating thoughts. The therapist can then look over these diary cards and help further customize the treatment process for their patient.

This will allow them to break free of their problems and stress. It may take time, as all treatment. But studies show that when both a therapist and patient put in the work, the results will show.

Eating Disorders and Negative Body Image

Since dialectic means to have two supposedly opposite viewpoints simultaneously, this can be especially helpful for people who have eating disorders. These people often struggle with all-or-nothing thinking that is black and white. They may think that they are a complete failure and worthless if they purge one day. But if these people are able to learn to look at it with a dialectic viewpoint, then they can learn to say "I *may have purged today, but I can continue to progress and work my way through recovery."*

People who don't live with an eating disorder or other mental health condition may assume that people with these disorders are simply not trying hard enough. Yet, most people suffering from mental illness including eating disorders are giving their absolute all in order to fight against their brain and cognition. They simply haven't had access to a treatment plan that works for them.

While eating disorders are destructive and greatly weigh on a person, by following the urges of the disorder they are able to feel a small amount of relief and distraction. Thankfully, with DBT, these people can learn more beneficial ways to find the same relief and comfort but in a healthy way for both their mind and body.

The use of DBT has been increasing for people with eating disorders because of its effective focus on healthy coping mechanisms and the regulation of emotions. By learning how to identify triggers, using tools such as breathing and relaxation exercises to manage stress, and practicing mindful eating, a person can greatly improve with the use of DBT. No matter the eating disorder, this therapy has been shown to help.

While cognitive behavioral therapy has been a long used and proven method to treat eating disorders and is often best to try first if someone doesn't have success with CBT, they may want to try DBT. Experts explain how DBT can help people with eating disorders similarly to how it helps people with a borderline personality disorder who self-harm. While the conditions are different, both consist of actions that cause the person harm. Yet, these harmful actions also give the person a sense of relief from their emotional pain. This explains why helping patients learn to regulate and communicate their emotions can lead to such success with both conditions.

Chapter 6: Benefiting from CBT and DBT in Daily Life

There are many benefits to using cognitive and dialectic behavioral therapies in your daily life. You can learn to better control your emotions, process grief, make informed decisions, release stress, understand other peoples' points of view, and more.

By learning these techniques, people can find a great improvement in their lives, whether they suffer from a mental illness such as anxiety disorder, depression, an eating disorder, PTSD, OCD, or any one of a number of other conditions. But even people who are mentally healthy can learn to better understand, communicate, and control their emotions, relax, and improve their lives with these techniques.

One of the most powerful ways in which you can improve your life, whether at home, work, school, or in your social life, is by using the cognitive or ABC model. We discussed this model early on in the book and it is as simple as filling out the following:

- Situation
- Mood

- Automatic Thoughts or Images
- Evidence that Supports these Thoughts
- Evidence that Disproves these Thoughts
- Alternative Healthy Thoughts
- New Mood

Whether you choose to fill these out in a journal, on your phone, or on pre-printed sheets of paper is up to you. The important aspect is to regularly use the cognitive model when you are experiencing negative thoughts or emotions such as stress, anxiety, depression, despair, anger, jealousy, or others.

Don't treat yourself in a way that you wouldn't allow anyone else to treat you. Nobody deserves to be constantly berated and attacked. It doesn't matter if the attack is coming from an outside source or themselves.

Breathing exercises are an important tool frequently used both with CBT and DBT because they have an incredible effect on calming the mind and body that is not possible with rest. There are many different exercises you can choose from and these can be done anywhere! If you are at work, school, or a party and find yourself becoming overwhelmed or struggling with a trigger, then you can try to find a secluded place to practice these breathing techniques.

The Four Seven Eight Method

This method is simple and takes very little time, allowing it to be done anywhere. While you can use this breathing exercise in any position when you first begin learning it, practice sitting with your back straight. You will need to place the tip of your tongue directly against the tissue behind your two upper front teeth. Be sure that your tongue stays in this position for the entire breathing exercise. While performing this exercise you will be exhaling through your mouth, but if it feels awkward to be exhaling around your tongue, you can try to slightly purse your lips.

- Begin by making a whooshing sound while completely exhaling through your mouth. Then close your mouth and count to four while you quietly inhale through your nose.

- Hold your breath to the count of seven and then once again, exhale completely. Be sure that you are holding your tongue in place and that when exhaling through your mouth, you are making a whooshing sound. While you exhale count to eight.

- This process is one breath and you will want to complete it for a total of four breaths.

It is important to note that while using this technique, you want to always audibly exhale through your mouth while quietly inhaling through your nose.

The exact time you spend on each phase does not have to be four, seven, and eight seconds. But you do need to be sure to keep this ratio of numbers. If you are having a difficult time holding your breath for seven seconds, then you can simply speed up the counting so that it is still the correct ratio but does not take a full seven seconds. As you practice this breathing exercise regularly, you will be able to adjust and slow it down.

This incredible breathing technique works similarly to a tranquilizer. Yet unlike tranquilizers, this method only increases in effectiveness the more you use it. While it may be tempting to do more than a four breath rotation of this at one time, be sure that during the first month, you always take a break between each set of four breaths. After the first month, you can increase it to eight, though you may find yourself lightheaded at first.

Try to practice this technique daily, preferably at least twice a day. If you ever find yourself in an overwhelming or triggering situation, you will find yourself familiar with this technique and ability to use it to help.

Breath Counting

This method is great if you find yourself needing time to meditate and relax in the morning before work, on your lunch break, or between classes. A few minutes of breath counting will clear your mind and ease any burden you may be carrying. Even if you don't feel stressed, after completing a session of breath counting, you will be astonished by how effective it is.

- Sit somewhere comfortable with your spine straight while keeping your head slightly inclined forward. Close your eyes and take a few deep breaths. Then allow your breathing to come naturally. Don't try to influence it. Although it is ideal if the breathing is quiet and slow, the rhythm and depth may vary from person to person.

- After your breathing becomes natural, count "one" as you exhale. The next exhale, count two and continue with this pattern until you reach five.

- After reaching five begin again at one and repeat this cycle for as long as you can. You may only complete this for three minutes, but ten minutes is preferable as this will help your mind and body reach a deeper state of relaxation.

You will know your mind and attention have been wondering if you notice yourself counting higher than five. Simply start over at one and keep up the one to five breath cycle. You want to continue focusing on your breathing, counting, and nothing else.

If we are struggling, it can be difficult to know what to do, but with the alternative action formula, we can easily work through the problem, how to manage the effects and ways that we can cope.

- First, begin by listing any difficulties or problems you may be experiencing. Follow it with a list of your vulnerabilities regarding the situation and your known triggers that are being affected.

- After you have clearly written out your problem and understand why you are experiencing it, then you can begin to list strategies for coping. These are not solutions to the problem you have, rather it is a way you can learn to manage the effects of the temporary impact caused by the problem. After you have your list of coping strategies, list their effects and how they make you feel. You want to write down both their advantages and disadvantage in the short-term and long-term.

- Lastly, write out actions you might take instead that could possibly resolve the problem.

Whether you are struggling with OCD, an eating disorder, depression, or anxiety, by using the alternative action formula, you can easily find ways to manage your triggers and better cope. If you find that this does not help you the first time, continue giving it an effort. It may take some people a little time to find coping mechanisms that work.

The functional analysis is a popular and well-used technique within cognitive behavioral therapy. This is because it can help many people learn about themselves. If you want to know more about your specific behaviors and what they lead to, then this technique may help.

- To begin this technique, separate a piece of paper into three sections. Write out a list of any behaviors that you wish to analyze in the leftmost column. These will most often be behaviors which are potentially problematic.

- In the center column, write out any factors that may have led to the behavior in question. These factors may apply either directly or indirectly.

- On the rightmost column of the page, write out any consequences that come as a result of the behavior that you are analyzing. While "consequences" may sound inherently negative, it does not have to be that way. In fact, some of the consequences could be quite positive.

Once you have completed the functional analysis, you will have a better understanding of your behavior and whether or not it will help you attain your goals. You will find that this can help you in every aspect of your life, as it can improve both your mental health and your relationships.

We all have unhelpful and unhealthy beliefs about ourselves and our behaviors, nobody is immune from this. On one hand, we may be our own worst critic, but on the other, we can be ignorant of the ways in which we can improve. Behavior experiments are a common tool in cognitive behavioral therapy, as they get us to question our thoughts and behaviors and learn if they are truly helpful or not.

To try out this technique, decide on a behavior that you want to analyze and then commit both to using that behavior and its opposite. For instance, you may think that you are more likely to work harder and focus better if you criticize yourself.

Therefore, first test yourself and see how you

work when you criticize yourself. Next, try being kind to yourself and see what you accomplish.

After you record the results of both criticizing and being kind to yourself, you can compare the two. This will give you an unbiased and honest view of whether your opinion is true or false.

Conclusion

You have learned much throughout this book, but you are not the sole person to have grown. Mary, Lydia, and Matt have all been making their own progress as well.

Mary had originally been in a constant state of depression. She was experiencing nightmares, listless during the day, unable to put her little energy into anything, distancing herself from loved ones, and frequently having thoughts such as *"Everyone is going to die and leave me behind,"* and *"What's even the point of living?"* It wasn't just painful for Mary, it was painful for everyone she cared about to see her going through such grief and unable to do anything about it.

But with the help of her psychologist, Mary learned to pick up techniques of cognitive behavioral therapy such as the cognitive model, deep breathing, functional analysis, and more. She even picked up on some dialectical behavior techniques in order to learn better acceptance of herself and her emotions.

After three months of cognitive behavioral therapy, Mary is doing much better and loving life again. She may occasionally have difficult moments, but she has learned to make use of her CBT toolkit to get her through them.

After Lydia's dream life had turned into a nightmare, she was out of options. She couldn't move away because she had signed a contract, but she was having daily overwhelming anxiety attacks. Even when she wasn't directly triggered by seeing or hearing a dog, she could begin to suddenly get anxious by just thinking about one.

After beginning therapy, she learned that she had to reduce her stress greatly. She began to do yoga, meditate, practice deep breathing, and she regularly used the cognitive model. While the change wasn't overnight, as soon as Lydia noticed she was beginning to improve, she decided to jump all the way in. She wanted to help her entire mind and body so she began eating a healthy diet, practicing better sleep hygiene, and exercising.

While exposure therapy wasn't easy at first, her therapist worked with her at her own pace so that she would feel as comfortable as possible. After beginning the process of imagining being around dogs, Lydia has finally managed to be around a large dog without having an anxiety attack. She wasn't comfortable, but she felt confident in the tools that her psychologist had provided her with. She had gained confidence by getting herself to this point.

While it was not originally easy for Matt to overcome his thoughts that therapy isn't for men, he soon learned all of the benefits it has to offer. In fact, Matt has found so much help from therapy and his psychologist that he is now a staunch supporter and recommends it regularly to people who are struggling.

It took time for Matt to become sober, but with the help of his psychologist, he learned new coping mechanisms, how to avoid triggers, and ways to manage his cravings. He even joined Alcoholics Anonymous and has made new friends there who understand his journey because they are on a similar one themselves.

Matt has also been using many techniques to control his emotions. Now, when he has anxious thoughts, rather than living in that state, he calms his mind, analyses the accuracy of the thoughts, and creates a new balanced thought. He has found this practice has also greatly improved his temper. He finds himself less often assuming people are demeaning him. And if he begins to get upset or angry, he practices breathing exercises before calmly and rationally analyzing the situation.

While the journey to change isn't an easy one, it is possible. While Matt originally thought he would only be happy with perfection, he has learned to embrace imperfection while still making progress toward his goal of a happy life free of alcohol and without uncontrollable anxiety and perfectionism.

There are many benefits to both cognitive and dialectical behavioral therapies. Whichever you choose or if you choose to combine the two, you can succeed. Whether your symptoms are mild and you are going on this journey on your own or your condition is more severe and you are using a trained professional as a guide, you can find benefit with CBT.

Even if you have previously attempted CBT and didn't improve, that doesn't mean you can't improve now. As long as you are willing to get help, be honest with yourself, and put in the effort, you can find the life you are hoping for. If you fail once, you can always try again. If you find that you aren't comfortable with a specific psychologist, then keep looking around your area until you find one that you are comfortable with. You can even find a trained psychologist or therapist to walk you through online therapy sessions.

There is no reason to continue living a life in which you are suffering or unhappy. You have access to all the tools you need to attain your dream of a happy life. Thank you for reading

Cognitive Behavioral Therapy. I hope that you have learned to forgive yourself, strive forward, and find support from those around you.

Lastly, if you enjoyed this book I ask that you please take the time to review it on Audible.com. Your honest feedback would be greatly appreciated.

Thank you.

Now, I would like to share with you a free sneak peek to another one of my books that I think you will really enjoy. The book is called "Mindfulness Meditation: A Practical Guide for Beginners" Published by Barrie Muesse Scott and Mark Davenport. It's an Introduction to Learn Meditation and Become Mindful Guided Meditation, Self Hypnosis, Subliminal Affirmations, Stress Relief & Relaxation.

Enjoy!

This book is all about using the power of your thoughts to be mindful and bring peace, purpose, and happiness to your life.

Drawing upon the rich tradition of Buddhism, mindfulness meditation is all about using your thoughts to be present in the moment and crafting the world that you want to live in. If you want to be more present in your daily life, this book is for you. If you want to heal and cope with chronic diseases, this book is for you. If you want to just sleep better or deal with your depression, then this book is definitely for you. Mindfulness meditation has been shown to have extraordinary effects on your life from your mental to physical health. This book will show you how to tap into the beautiful power of mindfulness meditation no matter if you are Buddhist or not.

The following chapters will discuss everything you need to know about embracing mindfulness meditation in your day-to-day life. However, an important distinction between mindfulness and meditation needs to be made before we proceed. Oftentimes, you see mindfulness and meditation used together. Other times, you may see mindfulness and meditations used interchangeably. Meditation is the more general term that refers to the practice of fine-tuning your mind through various mental exercises. Mindfulness is a form of meditation in which one focuses on being in the very moment compared to other types of meditation practices that may use chants or mantras. For the purposes of this book, it is important to note this distinction. Any meditation practice is great! However, this book will dwell on the importance of honing in on your breath with your mindfulness meditation practice.

Mindfulness Meditation: A Practical Guide For Beginners covers five chapters. In chapter 1, mindfulness meditation will be discussed thoroughly. How key concepts in mindfulness meditation relate to Buddhism, plus the benefits of mindfulness meditation, plus answers to frequently asked questions are included. The subject of chapter 2 is about how to practice mindfulness meditation. A practical guide about which positions are best and other best practices are highlighted. Chapter 3 explores more breathing and relaxation techniques that can be used to bolster your mindfulness meditation practice. The techniques in this chapter are able to help you vary your mindfulness meditation practice. Chapter 4 is dedicated to guided mindfulness meditation exercises that can help you as you begin your meditation practice. The scrips included will help you get started so you do not have to start your meditation practice from scratch. Chapter 5 is also dedicated to guided meditations, but the mindfulness meditation scripts in this chapter focus on guided meditations designed to heal various ailments.

This book about Mindfulness and Meditation will more than prepare you to begin your journey into mindfulness and meditation. There are a lot of famous people who practice mindfulness like Naomie Harris, Boris Johnson, Katy Perry, Richard Branson, and Anderson Cooper to name a few; thus, you are in great company.

There are plenty of books on this subject on the market, so thanks again for choosing this one! Every effort was made to ensure it is full of as much useful information as possible. Please enjoy!

Chapter 1: What is Mindfulness Meditation?

"To think in terms of either pessimism
or optimism oversimplifies the truth.
The problem is to see reality as it is."
– Thích Nhất Hạnh

How many times have we been encouraged to see the cup half full instead of half-empty? Oftentimes in western society, the push to be optimistic and to think positive is drilled into us from a young age. However, if one is beginning to become more mindful, the transition to mindfulness may feel a little jarring as it is opposite of what feels comfortable. Imagine this. Instead of focusing just on the positive aspect of life, mindfulness encourages a realistic outlook on life that embraces the good and the bad, the positive and the negative and the neutral. And this is where our book begins, starting off by learning about this effective way of living that has been used successfully for centuries – mindfulness meditation.

Buddhist monks have been using the power of mindfulness for over 2, 500 years. Mindfulness is the act of allowing your brain to rest while observing the thoughts that come and go in your mind. Mindfulness meditation is different from actively thinking and using your creative mind. When you are being mindful, you focus on an object, scene or sound that is calm and then let your thoughts gently amble by in your mind. Being mindful is powerful because if you are always caught up into being busy and always thinking about your next step, mindfulness gives you a much-needed break and makes you reflect on your pattern of thoughts and actions. It is the exact opposite of the daily living experience of most people because instead of going, mindfulness encourages you to slow down the pace.

Mindfulness allows you to know your thoughts instead of trying to change them. Instead of being judgmental and unkind to yourself if you think something negative, mindfulness has no judgment value on your thoughts. Your thoughts are just there. When you are mindful, you are taking notes of your thoughts like a note-taker. When you are in a mindful state, you just pay attention to what your thoughts are doing but giving them the freedom to do what they want. Ultimately, the goal of mindfulness is to know your mind. Once you begin to know your mind, you can begin the next step which is to train your mind.

The beautiful thing about our minds is that they are malleable, and as a result, they are trainable. Our minds are able to change based on what one is thinking. If you think the world is a horrible place, you will operate from a place of fear and your actions will show that. If you think that the world is a wonderful place, you will operate from a place of reckless optimism without being able to be realistic about certain dangers you may find yourself in. Mindfulness helps you to know your thoughts and then begin to train your thoughts to become more in tune with your long-term goals. Mindfulness slows down the grind of your busy daily pace and gives you a different vantage point about patterns in your life. These patterns can be feelings that you have in certain situations or your reactions to how other people treat you. When you are being mindful, you may notice trends and patterns that you are constantly thinking. Are you always wanting more and more? Do you feel comfortable with the way things are? Whatever patterns you notice, mindfulness can help you pinpoint what types of things are causing you mental, anguish, conflict, or joy. Then after noticing these patterns, you can begin to shape it to how you would like to be by focusing on being more gracious, compassionate, and kind with your thoughts.

When you begin your practice, do not treat your mindfulness meditation practices as an obligatory item on your daily to-do list. When you meditate, you want to be present in the moment, not treating the practice as an aggressive measuring stick to how fast you can change or using your meditation practice as a form of escapism without being willing to change your ideals. The most important thing to remember before you begin is that you are training your mind to be at peace with how things are going in the world, no matter what is happening. Once you are able to be at peace in no matter what situation you find yourself in, then you are able to start to work on yourself to change your values. Mindfulness meditation is not a sprint; it is a marathon that you continually work on until you are finally able to free yourself from unsavory emotions that are clinging to you whether they are anger, agitation, negativity, self-image issues, unfair, hasty judgments, and biased opinions and ideals.

When you are training your mind to be more mindful, affirmations are great tools to use. Affirmations are very helpful, especially when you create them yourself. The thought process behind using affirmations is to use very direct language which influences your subconscious to help you get the outcome that you want to get.

When you use affirmations, you want to first figure out what outcome it is that you want. Then create a short sentence with an active word. Make sure the sentence is in the present tense. For example, if you want to feel calmer and not be so anxiety-ridden, you can create an affirmation to help. You will start with the outcome of being calmer and make that into a statement using the present tense. Thus, the affirmation would be 'I am more calm.' By using the present tense, you are affirming the future outcome. When the affirmation is created, you can say it during your meditation time and throughout the day. When you couple this practice of saying affirmations with your mindfulness meditation session, they work doubly together to help you get the outcome that you want to get. For example, you hear the term think positive all the time. It is because positive thinking can help shape your future to where you have a positive future. However, if you think negative oftentimes a reality reflects your thoughts. Our thoughts influence our subconscious which in turn can determine our reality.

Mindfulness meditation helps you shape your reality by taking the time to know your mind. Once you know your mind, you will be able to train it and ultimately free it from negative, debilitating thinking. Every step works together.

Before you begin your mindfulness meditation practice, know that it is not going to be easy. It will be a journey, but if you are dedicated, you will see a difference in your life.

The History of Mindfulness Meditation

For Buddhists, nurturing mindfulness is the ultimate path to enlightenment. The point of Buddhism is to reach the highest truth by focusing on overcoming the limitations that your body has. Buddhists practice mindfulness by using four foundational truths of mindfulness. The four truths originate from a Buddhist sutta or sutra which is similar to a form of Buddhist scripture. The name of the sutta is called "The Discourse on the Establishing of Mindfulness" or the *Satipatthana sutta*. Please remember that the four establishments of mindfulness come from a very long and rich history. This book cannot possibly cover everything related to them, but hopes to serve as a general overview that can deepen your understanding of mindfulness meditation. The four truths are mindfulness of the body, mindfulness of feelings, mindfulness of consciousness and mindfulness of phenomena. Each foundation normally goes step-by-step in a flowing manner. You can go in and out of meditating upon each truth. They all work together. The first stop on the mindfulness journey is mindfulness of the body.

What is the one thing that you typically hear before beginning any form of meditation? The answer is watching your breath. Most meditation practices or guided meditations instruct you to begin by taking deep breaths in and exhaling deep breaths. Therefore, when you practice mindfulness, the first step is to think about mindfulness of your body. Initially, you'll want to start by being mindful of your breathing. Notice how deep or how shorts your breaths are when you start your meditation session. There are also different forms of body mindfulness you can focus on as well, such as mindfulness of eating or mindfulness of how you walk. These are some of the easiest mindfulness of the body to begin with, but we will focus on mindfulness of breathing since breathing is key to healing lots of ailments, physical and mental in your body.

Mindfulness of the body is just not about the positions your body is sitting in or how you breathe, eat and walk. Mindfulness of the body also involves a deeper understanding of how all your body parts work together. This includes how your leg connects to your thigh, how your ears function, or the power of body working throughout your body. Mindfulness of the body also seeks to understand some of the more unpleasant bodily functions such as urine or snot boogers or blood. The purpose of being mindful of your body is to reflect on how your body functions. You may ask, how do I try to be mindful of my body when I am meditating? An easy introductory way to do this is to imagine yourself greeting and thanking each body part for what it does. You can start at your feet and work your way up until you reach the top of your body.

The next foundation you should be concerned with when practicing mindfulness meditation is mindfulness of your feelings. A better way to explain mindfulness of your feelings is that this truth is concerned about being mindful of your neutral, painful, and pleasurable feelings. You can also reflect on how to be mindful of these feelings by using the senses of your touch, smell, hearing, seeing, taste, and your mind. In Buddhism, your mind is considered a sixth sense. It important to be mindful of these feelings because when you have painful feelings they can lead to fear and hatred. Too many neutral feelings can cause you to become disinterested and floated through life. When you are neutral about something, you are not concerned about it and as a result, it will not be important to you. Lastly, you have to be mindful of pleasurable feelings because too many pleasurable feelings can lead to lust and greed. It is important to be non-judgmental and only observe your thoughts, not acknowledge them when you meditate. The reason you do not want to acknowledge anything is that once you begin to acknowledge a thought as a neutral, painful or pleasurable feeling, you are in danger of attaching yourself to feelings that will prevent you from being enlightened. Thus, it is best to use mindfulness to observe when you are gaining feelings of neutrality, pleasure or painful so you know how to handle those feelings appropriately. When you practice mindfulness of feelings, you will still experience feelings.

Mindfulness of feelings does not mean that you do not feel. It only means that you are able to enjoy the feelings without going overboard to the point of the feelings cause you to become obsessed and overly attached to the thing that is causing the feeling, whether those feelings are good or bad. For example, if you love doughnuts and you find yourself obsessing over doughnuts, you can enjoy them so much that you want more and more doughnuts because of the pleasurable feeling that doughnuts give you. Eating too many doughnuts can cause issues your health like diabetes or chronic inflammation. All of these feelings started because of the seemingly innocent, yet pleasurable feeling of liking doughnuts. On the other side, if you are leery of a certain political leaning and it brings you immense pleasure, attaching yourself to that displeasure can quickly lead to hatred and biased feelings. However, if you are able to know your thoughts and know that this political leaning causes displeasure, you can work to be mindful that the political leaning is a trigger for you without attaching too much to that feeling to the point that it goes overboard. Likewise, if you feel neutral about a person, you can become so disinterested in them that you lose focus of the fact that they are human and worthy of respect. Hence, if they ever needed something, you would most likely overlook them or drag your feet to help them. So even feelings of neutrality can be dangerous. Once you become too attached to any type of feeling, the excess doting on the feeling prevents you from reaching enlightenment.

The next foundation of mindfulness meditation that you want to build upon is mindfulness of your consciousness. In Buddhism, there are 52 mental formations. Mental formations translated loosely are emotions and states of mind. The mental formations are normally grouped together in a specific way. The first of these formations are the previous feelings that were discussed in the mindfulness of feelings consisting of feelings of pleasure, neutrality, and displeasure. The next 51 formations are what the mindfulness of the consciousness helps you to focus on that are clustered in different groups. These include:

- Proficiency of mental properties

- Pliancy of mental properties

- Perception

- Composure of mind

- Appreciation

- Effort

- Righteousness of mind

- Worry

- Desire to do

- Amity

- Psychic life

- Error

- Perplexity

- Feeling

- Right livelihood

- Volition

- Initial application

- Attention

- Greed

- Buoyancy of mental properties

- Adaptability of mind

- Recklessness

- Right speech

- Sloth

- Discretion

- Proficiency of mind

- Modesty

- Conceit

- Right action

- Faith

- Buoyancy of mind

- Pliancy of mind

- Contact

- Deciding

- Concentration of mind

- Torpor

- Mindfulness

- Disinterestedness

- Envy

- Shamelessness

- Adaptability of mental properties

- Distraction

- Composure of mental properties

- Dullness

- Balance of mind

- Sustained application

- Pity

- Selfishness

- Reason

- Righteousness of mental properties

- Hate

This is a general overview of the mental formations, but you can study them in more detail to get a more detailed understanding. To simplify this foundation, when you are practicing mindfulness of the conscience, be observant of the different feelings that go in and out of your brain. To easily start meditating with mindfulness of the conscience, when you meditate observe any thoughts that you have. When your mind drifts from focusing on your breathing, you can call out to yourself that you are being mindful. When your mind begins to drift from not meditating, you can call out to yourself that you are not being mindful. This simple exercise is using mindful of your consciousness. It is also a great trick to use in your everyday life when you want to be more mindful.

The last foundation of mindfulness that you want to build upon is mindfulness of phenomena or mindfulness of perception. When you think of a car, you know it is an object that has four wheels and has the capacity to take you here and there. The idea that you have in your mind of a car may be realistic and based on a car that you know personally. Or the idea of a car that you may have can be based on what your perception of what a car is generally, according to your knowledge of what a car is. When you practice mindfulness of mental objects, you try to focus on the 'why' of how you perceive something. If you think of cars as positive, this positive association could be because of a childhood memory that when growing up you had a wonderful experience of your parents taking you to school every day in an old beat up, yet comfortable car. If you have a negative perception of cars, it could be because your friend was killed by a car or cars cause you to think of all the damage that they do to the ozone layer. Mindfulness of perception allows you to focus on the experiences that shape your perception of what something is so you can bypass those perceptions to get to the true meaning of what something actually is and not what you think something is.

When you practice mindfulness of perception, you want to be aware of things that can cause your perception to be tainted. These can be known as the 5 hindrances. You also want to be mindful of the 7 factors of awakening which should be what you aspire your perceptions to be based on. When all of these factors work together, it helps you eliminate suffering. The 7 factors of awakening that you want to focus on when you practice mindfulness of perception include:

- Equanimity – This factor can be described as the calm observance of things around you.
- Energy – This is the energy that powers you to lead the investigation to seek understanding about different topics in life.
- Concentration – The complete focus of the mind is what this factor seeks.
- Investigation of your perception – This factor encourages you to seek knowledge about phenomena to understand how something operates.
- Joy -Balanced pleasurable interest in something is what this factor is all about.
- Tranquility – Serenity and quietness encompass this factor.
- Mindfulness – Present moment awareness describes this factor.

The 5 hindrances to avoid are:

- Dullness – Doing your takes half-heartedly with no vim or lacking concentration.
- Lust – A craving for pleasure to fulfill all your senses.

- Ill will – Feelings of hatred directed to others.
- Restlessness and worry – This is when you are unable to calm your mind.
- Doubt – A lack of trust or conviction.

When you monitor your thoughts to see if any of the 5 hindrances appear in your train of thoughts, you want to note when and why they arose. You'll also want to note how you can prevent the hindrance from appearing again and how you can replace the hindrance with one of the 7 factors of awakening in their wake.

As you work on your mindfulness meditation, strive to attain the four foundational truths in the order of mindfulness of body, mindfulness of feelings, mindfulness of consciousness, and mindfulness of perception. This is ideal. However, you can meditate upon all of the foundations in one setting as well. So, if you focus on more than one truth at a time, that is ok as well. To truly attain enlightenment, you must find a way to master them all.

Lastly, mindfulness meditation helps you cultivate awareness of the "three characteristics of experience." According to Buddhism, if you do not understand these three characteristics, then you are bound to be caught up into an endless cycle of suffering. The three characteristics you should be aware of are the traits of impermanence, or *anitya*, dissatisfaction, or *duhkha*, and egolessness, or *anatma*. Impermanence means that all conditioned things will change. There is a constant change that you must be aware of. The next trait of dissatisfaction means that there is pain and suffering and no satisfaction in an unenlightened state. *Anatma* means that one should strive to act without an ego. These three are another aspect of Buddhist underpinnings behind the mindfulness meditation practice. These are great to keep in the back up your mind when you are doing mindfulness meditation.

Hopefully, up until this point, the case for why you practice mindfulness has been made. In case you still are not convinced, let's try to convince you one more time. So why mindfulness? There are lots of different meditation practices you can choose from, but mindfulness meditation is a great way to begin for a few different reasons.

Mindfulness is awesome because it:

- Helps you not be judgmental – One of the major components of mindfulness is to not be judgmental of yourself and others. This gentleness towards yourself improves your overall self-esteem. It also encourages self-compassion for yourself and for others.

- Easy and fast – There is no set time to do it. It is super easy to pick up on and relatively fast to do. Your sessions can be as long as they need to be or as short as they can be. If you have a busy schedule, you can meditate for 5 minutes or however long is best for you.
- Reduces stress instantly -Because the necessity of breathing is at the core of mindfulness meditation, deep breathing immediately reduces the stress you may be feeling as soon as you begin your mindfulness meditation session.
- Improves your wisdom – Mindfulness meditation improves your wisdom because you are able to figure out what makes you tick by noting and understanding the power of your thoughts. You also are able to be wise about other people, because this system meditation improves your observation skills such that you will be able to observe others and make connections about their behavior in ways that you have not been able to before.
- No set way to do it – For some people, the fact there is no set structure may be limiting to them, but it is a positive because there is not a right or wrong way to do it.

- Relaxing and calms your nerves – Just like reducing your stress instantly, mindfulness meditation also relaxes and calms your nerves due to the power of breathing.
- Observe yourself in the moment – Mindfulness meditation allows you to be in tune with your thoughts and actions so you are able to get into the 'zone' a lot easier than before.
- Easy to pick-up – Did I mention how easy mindfulness meditation is to pick up? Once you have one session, you will be able to do more rather easily.
- Doesn't have to depend on anyone else to do it – Mindfulness meditation is great to practice on your own. So you never have to worry about if the teacher is going to show up to class or not. This meditation style is self-guided so you can set your schedule according to your convenience.

Thank you, this preview is now over.

I hope you enjoyed this preview of my book "The Power of Mindfulness: Clear Your Mind and Become Stress Free" by Frank Steven. Please make sure to check out the full book on Amazon.com

Thank you.